Increasing Visual Literacy

In this digital age, the ability to process photographs, maps, charts, and graph[...]
journals—both online and in print—present information with some kind of vi[...]
high quality infographics and photographs to help students develop the ability to interpret and discuss visual
information.

STIMULATING INFOGRAPHICS from National
Geographic publications help explain complex
processes.

CHARTS, GRAPHS, AND TIMELINES
present information visually.

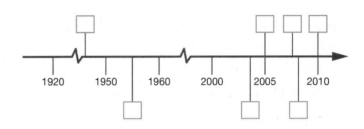

MAPS show locations and geographical features,
and illustrate historical facts and current trends.

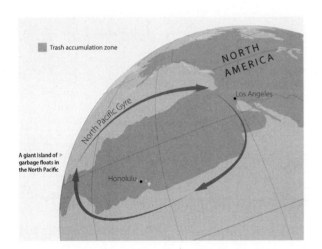

GRAPHIC ORGANIZERS show the relationships
between ideas in a visual way.

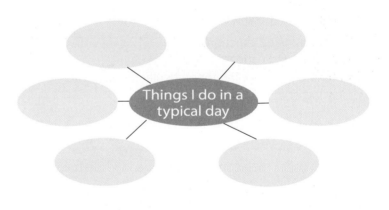

Using Videos

Pathways uses videos from National Geographic's award-winning film collection. The videos present a visually dynamic perspective of each unit's theme. Each video's narration has been carefully graded to match student proficiency levels.

Teaching Video Viewing Skills

Pathways promotes visual and digital literacy so learners can competently use a wide range of modern media. Videos differ from reading texts in important ways. Because students are processing more than just words, extra layers of meaning need to be understood:

- Information about the video's setting
- Signs and captions identifying people or places
- Maps and diagrams explaining information and processes
- Nonverbal communication such as facial expressions, gestures, and body language
- Music and sound effects

The transcripts for the videos can be found in the Teacher's Guide on pages 101–106.

The Video Section

Each unit features activities for students to do before, while, and after watching the video.

BEFORE VIEWING

This section provides background knowledge and stimulates interest in the topic by:

- predicting video content using images and captions.
- providing a short reading passage that includes background information about the topic.
- pre-teaching vocabulary from the video.

WHILE VIEWING

As they watch the video, students focus on:

- checking their predictions.
- identifying main ideas.
- watching and listening for particular details.
- inferring opinions and attitudes.

AFTER VIEWING

Students check their comprehension and relate the video to other aspects of the unit by:

- applying the ideas in the videos to their own lives and communities.
- synthesizing information from the video and information from the reading passages.

PATHWAYS

SECOND EDITION

1

Reading, Writing, and Critical Thinking

Teacher's Guide

COLLEEN SHEILS

NATIONAL
GEOGRAPHIC
LEARNING

Australia • Brazil • Mexico • Singapore • United Kingdom • United States

NATIONAL GEOGRAPHIC
L E A R N I N G

Pathways Teacher's Guide 1,
Reading, Writing, and Critical Thinking,
Second Edition

Colleen Sheils

Publisher: Andrew Robinson

Executive Editor: Sean Bermingham

Development Editor: Melissa Pang

Director of Global Marketing: Ian Martin

Product Marketing Manager: Tracy Bailie

Media Researcher: Leila Hishmeh

Senior IP Analyst: Alexandra Ricciardi

IP Project Manager: Carissa Poweleit

Senior Director of Production:
    Michael Burggren

Senior Production Controller: Tan Jin Hock

Manufacturing Planner: Mary Beth
    Hennebury

Art Director: Brenda Carmichael

Compositor: MPS North America LLC

Cover Photo: The Milky Way shines above
    sequoias in Yosemite National Park, USA:
    © Babak Tafreshi/National Geographic
    Creative

For product information and technology assistance, contact us at
Cengage Learning Customer & Sales Support, cengage.com/contact

For permission to use material from this text or product,
submit all requests online at **cengage.com/permissions**
Further permissions questions can be emailed to
permissionrequest@cengage.com

ISBN-13: 978-1-337-62483-1

National Geographic Learning
20 Channel Center Street
Boston, MA 02210
USA

National Geographic Learning, a Cengage Learning Company, has a mission to bring the world to the classroom and the classroom to life. With our English language programs, students learn about their world by experiencing it. Through our partnerships with National Geographic and TED Talks, they develop the language and skills they need to be successful global citizens and leaders.

Locate your local office at **international.cengage.com/region**

Visit National Geographic Learning online at **NGL.Cengage.com/ELT**
Visit our corporate website at **www.cengage.com**

Printed in the United States of America

Print Number: 01 Print Year: 2017

CONTENTS

TEACHING WITH *PATHWAYS*

In *Pathways*, real-world content from *National Geographic* publications provides a context for meaningful language acquisition. Each unit's high-interest content is designed to motivate both students and teachers alike. Students will learn essential vocabulary, review important grammatical structures, and practice reading and writing skills that will allow them to succeed in academic settings.

The features in each unit of *Pathways Reading, Writing, and Critical Thinking* include:

- *Academic Skills* listing at the start of each unit that highlights the unit objectives
- *Explore the Theme* pages that introduce the unit theme and key vocabulary
- Authentic readings that present target vocabulary and provide ideas for writing
- Audio recordings of all the reading passages
- *Grammar References* that present key structures and language for writing assignments
- *Vocabulary Extension* exercises that can be used in class or for self-study and review

The *Pathways* series is designed to be used in a wide variety of language-learning programs, from high schools and community colleges, to private language institutes and intensive English programs. Pacing guides for implementing the program in various teaching situations are provided on page xii.

Teaching Academic Literacy

In addition to teaching essential English language reading and writing skills, the *Pathways* series promotes other aspects of academic literacy that will help students succeed in an academic setting, such as:

- Visual literacy
- Critical thinking
- Classroom participation and collaboration skills
- The ability to use technology for learning

Students build essential academic literacy skills while encountering stories about real people and places around the world. The use of high-interest content from *National Geographic* publications builds global and cultural awareness, and develops learners' understanding of important 21st century issues that affect us all.

Building Critical Thinking Skills

Students today are expected to do more than just learn and memorize information. The ability to think critically about a topic—to analyze, evaluate, and apply ideas—is increasingly essential in an academic setting. *Pathways* actively fosters critical thinking while students read, listen, write, and discuss.

Critical Thinking and Language

Critical thinking requires a deep processing of language, which aids language acquisition. Articulating complex responses requires creative thought and word associations, which lead to better comprehension and retention of target language.

These are some of the critical thinking skills covered in *Pathways*:

- **Analyzing** Examining a text in close detail in order to identify key points, similarities, and differences.
- **Applying** Deciding how ideas or information might be relevant in a different context e.g., applying possible solutions to problems.
- **Evaluating** Using evidence to decide how relevant, important, or useful something is. This involves, for example, looking carefully at the sources of information, or the reasons the writer provides for or against something.
- **Inferring** "Reading between the lines;" in other words, identifying what a writer is saying indirectly, or implicitly, rather than directly, or explicitly.
- **Synthesizing** Gathering appropriate information and ideas from more than one source and making a judgment, summary, or conclusion based on the evidence.
- **Reflecting** Relating ideas and information in a text to your own personal experience and viewpoints, and forming your own opinion.

Each unit contains several opportunities for critical thinking. There is also an expanded *Critical Thinking* task in one of the *Understanding the Reading* sections:

> **CRITICAL THINKING**   Sometimes you can **evaluate** something using a set of criteria (factors). For example, when deciding how good a photograph is, you could consider things like the composition or lighting.

C Refer back to Annie Griffiths' ideas on the three elements necessary for a great photograph on page 182. Use the criteria to rate the photos. (1 = lowest score; 5 = highest score)

CRITICAL THINKING:
EVALUATING
USING CRITERIA

Photo	Composition	Moment	Light
gorilla			
pygmy ceremony			
Vietnamese family			

Frequently Asked Questions

How are the Student Book units organized?

Each unit consists of four main sections:

Reading 1, Video, Reading 2, Writing

The unit opens with an introduction to the unit theme. The reading passages and videos that follow, together with their corresponding exercises, build towards a final writing task that incorporates the skills, topics, and language presented in the unit.

Will my students be able to handle the themes in the book?

The content and language is graded so that students can come into the series with little or no background information.

Each unit starts with a *Think and Discuss* page. The questions get students thinking about the unit's theme. The *Explore the Theme* spread then formally introduces students to the theme. It makes use of short passages, statistics, infographics, and other images to ease students in.

As students progress through a unit, exercises and activities add further to students' knowledge of the theme. By the time students get to the writing task, they will have enough language and information to express in writing their own ideas about the topic.

How are *Readings 1* and *2* related?

The two readings offer different perspectives on the unit theme. They usually consist of contrasting text types, for example, one might be an explanatory magazine-type article with infographics, and the other an adapted interview. The variety of text types is designed to mirror the range of reading texts that learners will encounter in print and online.

How does the series build vocabulary skills?

Each reading passage contains eight to ten high-frequency vocabulary items (highlighted in blue). These are introduced in the *Preparing to Read* section, which focuses on developing students' ability to use contextual clues to determine meaning. Target words are then reinforced and recycled throughout subsequent units. In addition, *Vocabulary Extension* activities at the end of the Student Book expand on some of these target words by introducing useful collocations, highlighting different word forms, and presenting common prefixes, suffixes, and word roots.

How are reading and writing integrated in the series?

All of the sections and exercises in each unit are thematically linked. *Readings 1* and *2* and their corresponding activities present and reinforce ideas, vocabulary, and grammar that students will use in their *Writing Task*. For example, students may learn to understand pronoun reference in *Reading 1*, and then be taught to use pronouns to avoid repetition as part of the *Writing Task*. Or students may read about explorers in both reading passages, and then be asked to write about a place they would like to explore.

What is the writing process approach taken in this series?

Students learn early on that writing is re-writing. This is the premise of *Pathways'* process approach to writing. As students work through the pre-writing, writing, and post-writing activities in each unit, they draft and re-draft their assignments. By repeating this process as they progress through the units, students internalize the steps and gradually become more independent writers.

How does *Pathways* develop writing skills?

At the end of every unit, students complete a *Writing Task*. In Level 1, students are first asked to write connected sentences before progressing to writing full paragraphs in Unit 3.

A section called *Exploring Written English* helps to prepare students for the *Writing Task*, and contains the following features:

- The *Language for Writing* box highlights lexical or grammar points that are useful for that unit's writing task. Examples include using the simple present for describing routines and habits, and using expressions like *in addition* and *furthermore* to connect ideas in a paragraph.
- The *Writing Skill* box teaches useful sentence-level and paragraph-level writing skills. Early units explain simpler concepts like combining simple ideas to avoid short sentences and using synonyms to avoid repetition. Subsequent units include basic paragraph writing skills such as how to structure a narrative or an opinion paragraph.

The *Exploring Written English* section gives students the tools they need for their writing task, which they will perform in five stages:

Brainstorming, Planning, Drafting, Revising, Editing

Students are guided through these steps, working through a series of activities to help shape, structure, and fine-tune their writing. The *Revising* and *Editing* stages each include a guided practice task, using model examples. Students learn how to apply the principles in these practice tasks to their own writing.

The *MyELT* online workbook provides additional guided writing tasks that build on the skills and language that learners have developed in the Student Book unit.

Instructors may wish to refer to the Writing Assessment Rubric in the Teacher's Guide when assessing students' written work, or provide students with a copy of the rubric for them to do a peer assessment of their final drafts.

Pathways Reading, Writing, and Critical Thinking 1: Writing Assessment Rubric

Name: _____   Unit: _____

Criterion	Score of 4	Score of 3	Score of 2	Score of 1
Pre-writing and organization	☐ **Well organized** Units 1–2: • Supporting ideas are in a logical sequence Units 3–10: • Clear topic sentence • Supporting ideas are in a logical sequence • Strong concluding sentence	☐ **Good organization** Units 1–2: • Supporting ideas are in a mostly logical sequence Units 3–10: • Clear topic sentence • Supporting ideas are in a mostly logical sequence • Good concluding sentence	☐ **Some organization** Units 1–2: • Sequencing of supporting ideas is unclear Units 3–10: • Topic sentence is slightly unclear • Sequencing of supporting ideas is unclear • Weak concluding sentence	☐ **Lacks organization** Units 1–2: • Lack of sequencing of supporting ideas Units 3–10: • Weak topic sentence or lack of a topic sentence • Lack of sequencing of supporting ideas • No concluding sentence
Content	☐ **Excellent supporting ideas that are appropriate to the task** • Supporting ideas are well explained and have enough details • Supporting ideas are related to the task goal	☐ **Strong supporting ideas that are appropriate to the task** • Supporting ideas are somewhat explained with a bit of detail • Supporting ideas are mostly related to the task goal	☐ **Good supporting ideas, but some are slightly unrelated to the task** • Supporting ideas are incomplete with little detail • Some supporting ideas are unrelated to the task	☐ **Weak supporting ideas or ideas that are unrelated to the task** • Supporting ideas are weak with little or no detail • Supporting ideas are unrelated to the task
Vocabulary	☐ **Wide range of vocabulary** • Appropriate and related to task • Effective use of less common words • Errors are minor and not frequent	☐ **Good range of vocabulary** • Appropriate and related to task • Good attempt to use less common words • Occasional errors, but meaning is still clear	☐ **Average range of vocabulary** • Mostly appropriate and related to task • Some attempt to use less common words • A number of errors that affect understanding	☐ **Limited range of vocabulary** • Minimally appropriate and related to task • Inaccurate use of target vocabulary • Frequent errors that greatly affect understanding
Sentence Structure and Grammar	☐ **Excellent sentence structure and language use** • Varied sentence structure • Very few grammatical errors in subject-verb agreement, verb tense agreement, use of conjunctions, etc.	☐ **Good sentence structure and language use** • Good variety of sentence structure • A few grammatical errors in subject-verb agreement, verb tense agreement, use of conjunctions, etc. that do not affect understanding	☐ **Average sentence structure and language use** • Little variety in sentence structure • A number of grammatical errors in subject-verb agreement, verb tense agreement, use of conjunctions, etc. that slightly affect understanding	☐ **Weak sentence structure and language use** • Simple or repetitive sentence structure • Many grammatical errors in subject-verb agreement, verb tense agreement, use of conjunctions, etc. that greatly affect understanding
Spelling and Punctuation	☐ **Excellent command of spelling and punctuation** • Few or no spelling errors • Correct use of punctuation: ○ Capitalization of names and places and at the beginning of sentences ○ Use of comma between clauses and where appropriate ○ Use of period or question mark at the end of sentences ○ Use of apostrophes for indicating possession	☐ **Good command of spelling and punctuation** • Some spelling errors, but mostly with uncommon words • Mostly correct use of punctuation: ○ Capitalization of names and places and at the beginning of sentences ○ Use of comma between clauses and where appropriate ○ Use of period or question mark at the end of sentences ○ Use of apostrophes for indicating possession	☐ **Average command of spelling and punctuation** • A number of spelling errors, some with common words • Some incorrect use of punctuation: ○ Capitalization of names and places and at the beginning of sentences ○ Use of comma between clauses and where appropriate ○ Use of period or question mark at the end of sentences ○ Use of apostrophes for indicating possession	☐ **Weak command of spelling and punctuation** • Many spelling errors • Largely incorrect use of punctuation: ○ Capitalization of names and places and at the beginning of sentences ○ Use of comma between clauses and where appropriate ○ Use of period or question mark at the end of sentences ○ Use of apostrophes for indicating possession
Score				

Total score: ☐ / 20

USING THE TEACHER'S GUIDE

Each unit of this Teacher's Guide contains:

- Overviews of reading passages and videos
- Background information and key lesson points
- Teaching notes for each exercise
- Answer keys
- Follow-up questions and activities

Other features include:

Recommended Time Frames

Look out for the small clock icon with recommended times for completing various tasks. While the recommended total time required for each unit is about five class hours, this will of course vary depending on your particular teaching situation. Likewise, the time allocated for specific sections should be used more as a guide than as a rule. Refer to the pacing guides on the following page for a more detailed breakdown.

Ideas for…EXPANSION

These contain suggestions for extra classroom activities that can be used when students need additional support, or when there is an opportunity to explore a different aspect of the unit theme.

In addition, this Teacher's Guide also contains:

Video Transcripts

Use these for a more detailed study of the video content. The scripts, for example, can be provided to students after they view the video as additional reading practice.

Graphic Organizers

There is a photocopiable graphic organizer for one of the reading passages in the unit. The organizers include concept maps, process diagrams, and note-taking charts that can be handed out to students before or after they read the passage, to help them organize key points.

PACING GUIDES

One unit of *Pathways* typically requires 4.5–5 hours to complete. All ten units require approximately 45–50 hours.

By setting aside portions of each unit as homework, or by using extension activities and ancillaries, a *Pathways* unit can be adapted to suit various course durations. Here are some examples:

Total course length: 45 hours	Total course length: 60 hours	Total course length: 90 hours	Total course length: 120 hours
30-week course: 1 × 90 minute class per week	**30-week course:** 2 × 60 min classes per week **15-week course:** 4 × 60 min classes per week	**30-week course:** 2 × 90 min classes per week	**30-week course:** 4 × 60 min classes per week
1 unit = 3 classes (4.5 hours) 10 units = 30 classes	1 unit = 5 classes (5 hours) 10 units = 50 classes (out of 60 classes total) Remaining time = 10 hours *(Presentations / exams / reviews / school vacations)*	1 unit = 4 classes (6 hours) 10 units = 40 classes (out of 60 classes total) Remaining time = 30 hours *(group projects / presentations / exams / reviews / school vacations)*	1 unit = 8 classes (8 hours) 10 units = 80 classes (out of 120 classes total) Remaining time = 40 hours *(group projects / presentations / exams / reviews / school vacations)*
Class 1: Think and Discuss Explore the Theme Preparing to Read Reading 1 Understanding the Reading **Class 2:** Developing Reading Skills Video Preparing to Read Reading 2 **Class 3:** Understanding the Reading Exploring Written English Writing Task Unit Review	**Class 1:** Think and Discuss Explore the Theme Preparing to Read Reading 1 **Class 2:** Understanding the Reading Developing Reading Skills **Class 3:** Video Preparing to Read (vocabulary tasks) **Class 4:** Preparing to Read (predicting) Reading 2 Understanding the Reading **Class 5:** Exploring Written English Writing Task Unit Review	**Class 1:** Think and Discuss Explore the Theme Preparing to Read Reading 1 Understanding the Reading **Class 2:** Developing Reading Skills Video Preparing to Read Reading 2 **Class 3:** Understanding the Reading Exploring Written English **Class 4:** Writing Task Unit Review Extension activities	**Class 1:** Think and Discuss Explore the Theme Preparing to Read Reading 1 **Class 2:** Understanding the Reading Developing Reading Skills **Class 3:** Video **Class 4:** Preparing to Read Reading 2 **Class 5:** Understanding the Reading **Class 6:** Exploring Written English **Class 7:** Writing task Unit Review **Class 8:** Extension activities / group projects
This option assumes that: – the first draft, and the revising and editing of drafts, are set as homework.	This option assumes that: – the first draft, and the revising and editing of drafts, are set as homework.	This option assumes that: There is enough time to complete the entire Student Book and extension activities / Ideas for Expansion in class. – The Teacher's Guide provides numerous follow-up questions and extension activities in each unit. – Online Workbook activities and ExamView unit quizzes can be set as homework.	This option assumes that: There is enough time to complete the entire Student Book and extension activities / Ideas for Expansion in class. – The Teacher's Guide contains numerous follow-up questions and extension activities. – Online Workbook activities and ExamView unit quizzes can be done in class or set as homework.

ACADEMIC SKILLS

READING	Skimming for gist
WRITING	Writing good sentences
GRAMMAR	Simple present tense
CRITICAL THINKING	Inferring meaning

UNIT OVERVIEW

The theme of this unit is daily life and how it differs across countries and cultures. From the lives of regular people and National Geographic Explorers, students learn and discuss what goes on in the world every day.

- **READING 1:** A film documents the lives of people from all around the world on a single day in 2010.

- **VIDEO:** Teens from various countries and cultures Skype one another to share and learn about one another's daily lives.

- **READING 2:** In an interview, three National Geographic Explorers discuss their everyday lives and the highs and lows of their jobs.

Students draw on what they've read and watched to write effective sentences about their daily lives. The unit prepares them by introducing vocabulary to talk about activities, teaching when and how to use the simple present tense, and offering three tips for writing good sentences. Lastly, the unit introduces students to brainstorming and using an outline to prepare drafts—skills that students will use in every unit's *Writing Task*.

THINK AND DISCUSS *(page 1)*

The scene depicts a typical day on a busy street in Karachi, Pakistan. It is meant to show students a typical day that probably looks very different from their own.
- Have students study the picture, title, and captions.
- Discuss the photo as a class. What do students think the photo and the unit are about? Provide your own overview.
- Discuss the questions as a class. Ask students to reflect on their own daily lives, stressing the word *daily*.

THINK AND DISCUSS

Answers will vary. Possible answers:

1. Sunday is my favorite day because I can relax and spend time with my friends or family. / I love Monday because I like starting a new week. / My least favorite day is Thursday because I have to take a test every Thursday. / I always work late on Monday, so that's my least favorite day.

2. I enjoy having breakfast every morning. It's my favorite meal of the day. I usually have scrambled eggs, toast, and a cup of tea. / I like catching up with my friends on social media. I don't get to meet them so often anymore, but I'm able to chat with them on social media sites.

EXPLORE THE THEME *(pages 2-3)*

Students will read statistics about a few things that happen every day on Earth. First, point out the numbers at the bottom of page 2. *One thousand* has three zeros, *one million* has six, and *one billion* has nine.
- Allow students time to study the spread and answer the questions individually.
- Check answers as a class. For question **1**, have students compare the answers to the populations of their own towns, cities, or countries. Are students surprised by the numbers?
- Elicit sample sentences from students for each of the blue words.

EXPLORE THE THEME

A **1.** The world's population grows by about 200,000 people every day. More than eight million fly to a different place daily. More than one billion people visit Facebook every day.

  2. Answers will vary. Possible answers: Yes, I use the Internet every day. I check my email, chat with my friends, post pictures online, do research for school, and watch videos.

B   connect; communicate; upload (Note: The verb *connect* can refer both to communicating with others in an online environment and the act of getting online itself.)

Reading 1

PREPARING TO READ *(page 4)*

30 MINS

A Building Vocabulary

Building Vocabulary exercises introduce students to key vocabulary items from the reading passage. Students should find the blue words in the passage and use contextual clues to guess the meanings of the words and phrases. One useful clue is part of speech. For example: Nouns are often preceded by articles such as *a* or *the* (*a team, the project*); verbs often take the infinitive form (*to produce, to communicate*); adjectives frequently appear after forms of the verb *be* (*is normal, are extraordinary*). Recognizing parts of speech can help students understand new words better.

- Have students complete the exercise individually.
- Check answers as a class. Ask students for the part of speech of each blue word or phrase. What other clues from the reading passage did students find helpful?
- Elicit sample sentences for each vocabulary item.

See Vocabulary Extension 1A on page 203 of the Student Book for additional practice with "-ion" extensions for verbs ending with the letters t *and* s *(connection, discussion).*

B Using Vocabulary

Students should practice using the new vocabulary items while answering the two questions.

- Have students work in pairs to answer the questions.
- Check answers as a class. Elicit sample answers from students. For question **1**, ask students if they know how people communicated before the Internet was available. For question **2**, do students think people's typical days have changed much over the years?

Ideas for… EXPANSION

A vocabulary notebook is a great way for students to build their vocabularies. Demonstrate on the board how to write new words in the notebook; include details such as *part of speech, meaning, translation,* and an *example sentence.* (Example: *arrive [verb]: to reach a place. "I arrived at school just before my first class."*)

C Brainstorming

Students should briefly list activities that they think most people around the world do every day. Offer students one or two examples (*eat dinner, exercise*).

- Allow students time to complete the activity individually.
- Have them discuss their answers in pairs.

- Discuss as a class. Create a large mind map on the board. Do people around the world really do these things every day?

D Scanning/Predicting

Predicting what a passage is about before reading it helps the reader understand the passage better later. Scanning for key details is a good way to predict what a passage is about. In this reading passage, the numbers in the first paragraph offer readers some useful insight.

- Allow students time to scan the first paragraph for numbers. Stress that students should scan quickly and not read the entire paragraph.
- Have them discuss their answers in pairs.
- Discuss the most probable answer as a class. Revisit this question after completing the reading to see whether students guessed right.

ANSWER KEY

PREPARING TO READ

A **1.** extraordinary

   2. arrive

   3. team; project (Note: A *project* is something that usually takes a long time to finish.)

   4. normal (Note: Students will also see the synonym *typical* in the reading.)

   5. take care of (Note: *Taking care of* someone means looking after that person's health and well-being.)

   6. produce (Note: *Produce* is often used instead of *make* for larger, more complicated projects or items.)

B   Answers will vary. Possible answers:

   1. I usually communicate with my family by phone. They don't like texting very much. I communicate with my friends by texting, mostly. Text messages don't interrupt as much when we're in class or at home doing our homework.

   2. On a normal weekday, I eat breakfast early in the morning before taking the subway to school.

C   Answers will vary. Possible answers: exercise / eat breakfast / drink coffee / take the train / drive to work / walk home / cook dinner / take a bath

D   c (Note: Numbers include the year the movie was made [2010], the date the videos were recorded [July 24], the number of videos made [80,000], the amount of video recorded [4,500 hours], the number of countries that participated [192], and the final length of the edited movie [90 minutes].)

OVERVIEW OF THE READING

The passage describes the making of the movie *Life in a Day*. The movie was made from videos that people all over the world submitted showing what they did on a specific day—July 24, 2010. The film's director, Kevin Macdonald, also asked contributors to talk about their loves and fears. The final film shows both our cultural differences and the many ways in which we are the same. The full 90-minute movie can be viewed online.

Online search terms: Life in a Day, Kevin Macdonald

UNDERSTANDING THE READING
(page 7)

A Understanding Main Ideas

A passage usually contains several main ideas. This question asks students to determine one of them: the main purpose of the *Life in a Day* project. Point out that this is not the only main idea in the passage. Other main ideas in the passage include how the project was conducted and what the project revealed.

• Have students answer the question individually.
• Check answers as a class. Ask students where they found the answer.

B Understanding Details

The details in this exercise expand on the main purpose of the *Life in a Day* project.

• Have students complete the exercise individually.
• Have them check their answers in pairs.
• Discuss as a class. Ask students where they found their answers.

C Critical Thinking: Inferring Meaning

The *Critical Thinking* box explains how to guess the meaning of words using context. You would have already covered this with students in *Preparing to Read*, but go over the lesson again because inferring meaning is a useful skill that will be practiced throughout the book. Ask why inferring meaning can be better than using a dictionary. Explain that stopping to look up a word halfway through a passage can affect reading fluency and interfere with comprehension. Exercise **C** offers student more practice with this skill, this time with more

challenging words. Students need to locate the words in the reading and pay close attention to the words around them.

• Have students complete the task individually.
• Check answers as a class. Ask students what clues they used to arrive at their answers. Elicit sample sentences for each word.

D Critical Thinking: Applying

Students should process the information in the passage to determine which parts of their lives they want to film and submit. What would the director want to see in students' videos? Draft a sample answer for students before the exercise.

• Have students complete the task individually.
• Have them discuss their answers in pairs.
• Discuss as a class. Elicit sample answers, and vote for the idea most likely to be included in the film.

ANSWER KEY

UNDERSTANDING THE READING

A c (See Paragraph A: *What happens in a single day on planet Earth?*)

B 1. b (See Paragraph A: *The team asked people from around the world to film their life…*)

2. a (See Paragraph C: *What we might see as banal, living in our own culture, is not banal to somebody growing up in Dakar.*)

3. a (See Paragraph E: *…you can ask thousands, tens of thousands, maybe hundreds of thousands of people all to contribute to a project…*)

4. b (See Paragraph F: *The* Life in a Day *team hopes that, after watching the movie, others may feel the same way.*)

C 1. goes on

2. imaginary

3. banal

4. contribute

D Answers will vary. Possible answers: I would send a video of my family eating dinner together because we always laugh and joke together. / I would send a video of one of my classes because I think students are interested in seeing other schools around the world.

DEVELOPING READING SKILLS *(page 8)*

Reading Skill: Skimming for Gist

The *Reading Skill* box explains that skimming is a quick way to determine the general idea of a passage, or its gist. In daily life, we skim text frequently to decide whether a passage is useful. For example, we may quickly skim through many articles online before choosing one that suits our purpose. When skimming a reading, students should not read every word. They should instead look out for titles, subtitles, headings, and repeated words. Photos, captions, charts, and other graphics are also useful.

A Skimming for Gist

The key words that students should pay attention to while skimming are already highlighted in the paragraph. Tell students not to read the paragraph. Instead, they should read only the highlighted words before choosing their answer.

- Have students skim the paragraph and complete the exercise individually.
- Elicit sample answers from students. Then have them read the passage carefully and revise their answers, if necessary.
- Check answers as a class. Ask who managed to get the answer right the first time. Which highlighted words did they find useful?

B Skimming for Gist

In this exercise, key words are not highlighted in the paragraph for students. While skimming, students need to notice for themselves key words or ideas that are repeated.

- Have students skim the paragraph and complete the exercise individually.
- Elicit sample answers from students. Then have them read the passage carefully and revise their answers, if necessary.
- Check answers as a class. Ask who managed to get the answer right the first time. Which words did they find useful?

ANSWER KEY

DEVELOPING READING SKILLS

A a (Note: Students should notice that the words *hours* and *days* are repeated a lot. They should also notice the names of the different planets.)

B c (Note: Students should notice some of the following key words and phrases: *first baby, typical day, different, sleep, awake, time, feeding, diapers, tired, happiness.*)

Video

VIEWING: A GLOBAL CONVERSATION *(pages 9–10)*

Overview of the Video

A group of teenagers in the city of Philadelphia, U.S.A., chat online with teens from Kazakhstan, France, and Nigeria. They meet using Skype and ask one another questions about their lives and experiences. They discuss the things that are unique about the places where they live, but they also get to see how much students around the world have in common. This video showcases the educational program *Do Remember Me*. The video was adapted from the short film *The World Is as Big or as Small as You Make It*. Students can watch the full 11-minute version of the film online.

Online search terms: Do Remember Me, The World Is as Big or as Small as You Make It, Teens from Around the World Skype Each Other, This Is What Happens

BEFORE VIEWING

A Predicting

Predicting the video content helps students understand it better when they view it. The title suggests that the people in the photo are not just watching something. They are in a global conversation, so they are probably talking to people from different countries. The scene looks like a classroom, and the young people are probably students. They are accompanied by a single adult, probably their teacher. The students in the photo are probably talking to other students from around the world.

- Allow some time for students to study the title, photo, and caption.
- Discuss as a class. Elicit sample answers from students.

B Learning About the Topic

The paragraph prepares students for the video by describing the project *Do Remember Me*.

- Allow students time to complete the exercise individually.
- Discuss as a class. Elicit sample answers. Ask whether students have had similar experiences communicating with others online and whether they would enjoy participating in a project like *Do Remember Me*.

C Vocabulary in Context

This exercise introduces students to some of the key vocabulary items used in the video. Students should use contextual clues to deduce the meanings of the words.

- Have students complete the exercise individually.
- Check answers as a class. Elicit sample sentences for each word.

BEFORE VIEWING

A Answers will vary. Possible answers: I think that they're talking to teens from another country. The title says "conversation," so they're probably not talking to a teacher or professor. That would be more like a lecture.

B Answers will vary. Possible answers:

1. Students will learn that they have a lot in common with people from other countries. This will help them to get along better with one another.

2. Skype is free and easy to download. You can also use Skype on any computer, tablet, or mobile phone.

3. I think students would probably ask each other about everyday things, such as the food they eat, the schools they attend, and the hobbies they enjoy.

C 1. alike

2. amaze (Note: Something that is *amazing* is both unexpected and very impressive.)

3. exchange (Note: People can *exchange* intangibles such as ideas, as well as actual things.)

WHILE VIEWING

A ▶ Understanding Main Ideas

Have students read the items before you play the video.
- Have them complete the task while the video is playing.
- Check answers as a class.

B ▶ Understanding Details

Have students read the questions and write any answers they recall from the first viewing before playing the video a second time.
- Have students complete the task while the video is playing.
- Check answers as a class. Ask students which country and conversation was the most interesting and why.

WHILE VIEWING

A 1. their daily lives

2. recording videos of themselves

3. that people are more similar than different

B 1. d; 2. c; 3. b; 4. a (Note: To *beatbox* is to make drum sounds with the mouth. It is strongly connected to hip-hop culture.)

AFTER VIEWING

A Reacting to the Video

Question **1** asks students to explain the quote that is also the title of the film from which the video was adapted. Ask students to think about what the world being big or small means. For question **2**, ask students to imagine themselves as participants in one of the conversations.
- Have students answer the questions in pairs.
- Discuss as a class. For question **1**, elicit sample answers. Write down a promising answer, and ask students to modify it to make it more precise.
- For question **2**, elicit sample answers and list them on the board. Have students answer the questions themselves to see how similar or different their answers are.

B Critical Thinking: Synthesizing

Students draw on information from both Reading 1 and the video to *synthesize* their answers.
- Allow students time to answer the question in pairs.
- Discuss as a class. Elicit sample answers and list them on the board.

AFTER VIEWING

A Answers will vary. Possible answers:

1. In a big world, everyone seems far away and hard to connect with. In a small world, we are all connected and we realize that our similarities are greater than our differences. We decide for ourselves which of these worlds we live in.

2. What do you eat for breakfast? / What language do you speak at home? / What do you like to do in your spare time?

B Answers will vary. Possible answers: Both projects are made possible by the Internet. / Both projects expose people to different cultures around the world (Note: While technology and language are important parts of these projects, the main similarity is that they both promote cultural exchange and highlight similarities around the world.)

Reading 2

PREPARING TO READ *(page 11)*

A Building Vocabulary

Students complete the sentences with key vocabulary words from the passage. Point out that students need to use the correct form of the words. Ask students to use contextual clues from the passage to infer the meaning of the words, if necessary.

- Have students complete the exercise individually.
- Check answers as a class. Elicit sample sentences for each vocabulary item.

See Vocabulary Extension 1B on page 203 of the Student Book for additional practice with various collocations of the word time *(save time, waste time).*

B Using Vocabulary

Students should use the new vocabulary items while answering the two questions.

- Have students work in pairs to answer the questions.
- Check answers as a class. Elicit sample answers from students.

C Brainstorming

This exercise gets students thinking about interesting jobs, which is what the reading passage is about. For question **1**, they should think of at least three jobs and the reasons they are interesting. Ideas should be brief. Provide one or two examples, if necessary.

- Have students answer the questions individually.
- Have them discuss their answers in pairs.
- Discuss as a class. Elicit sample answers from students. List the more unusual jobs on the board, and ask students whether they would enjoy those jobs.

D Predicting

Although each Explorer's job is clearly labeled in the photo captions, students may not understand what the labels mean. If students need more clues, ask them to skim the first sentence of each section that summarizes the work each person does.

- Allow students time to skim through the pictures and captions.
- Discuss as a class. Revisit the activity after completing the reading.

ANSWER KEY

PREPARING TO READ

A 1. depends on (Note: Students should use *depends*, not *depend*.)
2. balance, spend time
3. during
4. surprise
5. realize
6. schedules (Note: Students should use the plural form of the word.)
7. measure

B Answers will vary. Possible answers:
1. During my free time, I enjoy hanging out with my friends / going to the movies / playing video games with my brother.
2. I spend most of my free time reading. / Most of my free time is spent surfing the Internet. / I spend a lot of my free time practicing the piano.

C Answers will vary. Possible answers:
1. I think being an actor is interesting. You get to play a lot of different roles. / Being an astronaut is interesting because you get to work in zero gravity.
2. Scientist / Musician / Travel writer / Social worker / Athlete

D 1. c (Note: Katija is a bioengineer.)
2. b (Note: Lee is a bioarchaeologist.)
3. a (Note: Qi is a filmmaker and a photographer.)

🎧 **2** Have students read the passage individually, or play the audio and have students read along.

OVERVIEW OF THE READING

Three National Geographic Explorers talk about their work. They give a description of their jobs and where they work, describe a typical day, talk about the highs and lows of their jobs, and share some interesting stories. National Geographic has a number of Explorer programs that recognize and support uniquely gifted and inspiring scientists, conservationists, storytellers, and innovators who are making a difference and changing the world.

Online search terms: National Geographic Emerging Explorers Program, Kakani Katija, Christine Lee, Ricky Qi

UNDERSTANDING THE READING
(page 14)

A Understanding Main Ideas

Students select the option that best summarizes the point of the passage.

• Have students answer the question individually.
• Check answers as a class. Ask students where they found the passage's purpose.

B Understanding Details

Venn diagrams are useful tools for comparing similarities and differences. In this three-circle Venn diagram, students decide whether each detail applies to only one person, to two people, or to all three. Do items a and b with the class.

• Allow students time to fill in the rest of the items individually.
• Check answers as a class. Ask students where they found the relevant information.

C Critical Thinking: Inferring Meaning

Go over with students again the gist of the *Critical Thinking* box that appeared earlier in the unit. Students should use contextual clues from the passage to figure out what the words mean. Some words appear more than once in the passage.

• Have students complete the exercise individually.
• Check answers as a class. Elicit sample sentences for each word.

D Critical Thinking: Reflecting

To *reflect* is to imagine yourself in a story or situation, so as to deepen your understanding of it. Encourage students to imagine themselves working in each of the Explorers' jobs while completing the exercise.

• Have students complete the exercise individually.
• Have them discuss their answers in pairs.
• Discuss as a class. Elicit sample answers. Which, if any, of the jobs would students like to have? Vote as a class to decide which Explorer has the best job.

UNDERSTANDING THE READING

A   b (Note: The purpose can be found in the sentences just below the title. Explain the slight difference between options a and b. Option a is about a specific day, whereas b is about a typical day.)

B **a.** Lee
   b. Katija, Lee
   c. Katija
   d. Qi
   e. Qi, Katija, Lee
   f. Qi
   g. Katija, Lee
   h. Katija

C **1.** quit (Note: *Quit* also frequently means to choose to leave a job.)
   2. buried
   3. skeleton (Note: Christine Lee is pictured handling a skeleton on page 13.)
   4. dive
   5. laboratory

D   Answers will vary. Possible answers:

   Katija: Diving in the ocean

   Lee: Making new discoveries

   Qi: Traveling around the world

   I think Kakani Katija has the most interesting job. Diving in the ocean sounds fun and exciting. / I've always liked history, so I think Christine Lee has the most interesting job.

Ideas for… EXPANSION

Have students pair up and role-play an interview similar to the ones in the passage. Interviewers should ask the same questions, while interviewees should answer as if they were working in the dream jobs they listed in exercise **C** of *Preparing to Read*. Have students switch roles so that everyone gets a chance to be interviewed.

Writing

OVERVIEW

In this section, students learn to write sentences about daily activities using the simple present tense. The lesson starts by walking students through the uses of the simple present tense. It then teaches students three simple tips for writing good simple present tense sentences. In the *Writing Task*, students apply these lessons by writing sentences describing three of their daily activities that someone from a different country would find interesting. Students begin with a brainstorming exercise. They then learn how to select, organize, and combine ideas in an outline before preparing a draft. Finally, they learn how to improve their drafts and check for common mistakes with the simple present tense.

 EXPLORING WRITTEN ENGLISH
(pages 15–17)

A Noticing

While completing the exercise, students are expected to notice that the simple present tense can be used for both general facts and routines. This exercise is to be done before going over the information in the *Language for Writing* box.

- Have students complete the task individually.
- Check answers as a class. Ask students what all the sentences have in common.

Language for Writing: Simple Present Tense

The *Language for Writing* box explains that for both routines and general facts, students should use the simple present tense. Routines include habits and things that happen regularly. General facts are statements that are true, or believed to be true. For the writing task, students will most likely focus on routines.

B Language for Writing

Students practice using the correct simple present form of each verb. Remind students that they need to identify the subject to get the verb form correct.

- Have students complete the task individually.
- Check answers as a class. Ask students to name the subject for each verb.

C Language for Writing

Each question requires an answer describing a routine or general fact.

- Have students answer the questions individually.
- Have them check answers in pairs.
- Discuss as a class. Elicit sample answers from students, and write them on the board. Name the subject in each sample answer, and ask students to point out any errors.

See Grammar Reference on pages 219–223 of the Student Book for additional information on the simple present tense.

ANSWER KEY

EXPLORING WRITTEN ENGLISH

A **1.** GF
 2. GF
 3. R
 4. R
 5. GF

LANGUAGE FOR WRITING

B **1.** communicate
 2. are (Note: Explain that *are* is a form of the verb *be*.)
 3. is (Note: Explain that *is* is another form of the verb *be*.)
 4. works, does, work
 5. have, has
 6. take

C Answers will vary. Possible answers:
 1. My favorite hobby is playing video games.
 2. I like going to the beach.
 3. My favorite movie is *Inception*.
 4. I spend time with my friends on weekends.
 5. I take the bus and walk the rest of the way.
 6. I study at a high school.
 7. My family enjoys going to the movies.

Writing Skill: Writing Good Sentences

The *Writing Skill* box offers three simple tips for writing good simple present tense sentences: The sentence should include a subject and a verb; the subject and verb should agree; simple ideas should be combined to avoid repetition.

D Writing Skill

Students should refer to the three tips and edit the sentence or sentences in each item.

- Allow students time to complete the task individually.
- Check answers as a class. Ask which rule was broken for each item.

E Writing Skill

Students use the three tips to write sentences about their favorite weekend activities. The sentences need not be related.

- Allow students time to complete the task individually.
- Have them check their answers in pairs.
- Discuss as a class. Elicit sample sentences from students.

F Writing Skill

Students should form groups of three and discuss their favorite weekend activities. They should write one sentence describing each student's favorite activity, and another sentence comparing this favorite activity to their own. Write a sample answer on the board for students to refer to.

- Allow students time to complete the activity in groups.
- Discuss as a class. Elicit sample answers from students.

ANSWER KEY

WRITING SKILL

D 1. I work in an office <u>on</u> First Street.

2. My friend and I like to <u>play</u> computer games.

3. My best friend's name <u>is</u> John.

4. <u>My favorite movie is</u> *Iron Man*.

5. My family likes to go hiking <u>in the mountains in the summer</u>.

6. We <u>eat</u> dinner at 7:00 every evening.

7. One of my favorite sports <u>is</u> basketball.

E Answers will vary. Possible answers:

1. I love to surf, so I go to the beach every weekend.

2. I meet up with members of my band every weekend for practice.

3. Every Sunday, my family shares a big meal.

F Answers will vary. Possible answers:

Jim enjoys exercising, and he hikes every Saturday. I like exercising, but I prefer playing sports. I think hiking is boring. / Sharon goes for salsa classes with her friends every weekend. I like to dance, too, but I prefer hip-hop.

WRITING TASK *(page 18)*

A Brainstorming

Brainstorming is a useful first step for gathering ideas before writing. Read the *Goal* box aloud so students can become familiar with the writing task before brainstorming. The aim is to describe three activities that would be interesting to people from other countries. When brainstorming, students should list as many ideas as possible without worrying too much about how good the ideas are, as long as they are on topic. Ideas should be briefly worded. They need not be listed in any order.

- Allow students time to complete the task individually.
- Have students share their ideas in pairs and offer feedback to each other.

B Planning

After brainstorming, the next step is to select the best ideas. Then students organize their information. This is made easier with an outline, such as the one in the exercise. Students arrange their ideas and add details to each one. Remind students that complete sentences are not necessary. It is more important to focus on selecting and organizing their information.

- Allow students time to complete their outlines individually. Provide assistance as needed.

C First Draft

Have students write first drafts of their sentences, based on their outlines.

- Allow students time to complete the task individually. Provide assistance as needed. Refrain from error correction at this point.

ANSWER KEY

WRITING TASK

A Answers will vary. Possible answers: drink tea / exercise / walk my dog / call my parents / cycle to school / go running

B Answers will vary. Possible answers:

1. Prepare breakfast: Normally noodles with a fried egg, sometimes with vegetables.

2. Help out at my father's shop: My father fixes motorcycles, the main mode of transportation here.

3. Play soccer with friends: No soccer fields here, so we play on basketball courts.

REVISING PRACTICE (page 19)

Explain to students that first drafts are never final drafts. Students should always look for ways to revise and improve their first drafts. The *Revising Practice* box contains an exercise that demonstrates several ways students can improve their first drafts.

- Allow students time to analyze the two drafts and complete the exercise.
- Check answers as a class. Ask students to identify each change and explain how it makes the revised draft stronger.

D Revised Draft

Students should apply the revision techniques used in the *Revising Practice* box to their own drafts, where applicable.

- Explain to students that they will be using the questions as a guide for checking and improving their drafts.
- As a class, go over the questions carefully to make sure students understand them.
- Allow students time to revise their sentences.

EDITING PRACTICE

The final step after revising a draft is to check thoroughly for errors and correct them. The *Editing Practice* box trains students to spot and correct common errors related to the simple present tense. As a class, go over the information in the box carefully to make sure students understand what to look out for.

- Allow students time to complete the exercise individually.
- Check answers as a class by asking students to read their corrected sentences aloud and explain the errors.

ANSWER KEY

REVISING PRACTICE

a, b, d, b, c

EDITING PRACTICE

1. I <u>cook</u> food for 500 people every day.
2. I think many people <u>don't</u> cook nowadays.
3. My husband <u>drives</u> me to work every morning.
4. He <u>is</u> a bus driver.
5. I don't <u>work</u> in an office.
6. I <u>work</u> in a laboratory.
7. My grandparents <u>don't</u> watch TV.
8. My daughter doesn't <u>have</u> a job. (Note: The tense is reflected in the auxiliary verb *do*.)

E Final Draft

Have students apply the skills taught in *Editing Practice* to their own revised drafts and check for any other errors.

- Allow students time to work individually on editing their drafts.
- Walk around and monitor students as they work. Provide assistance as needed.
- Collect their work once they have completed it.
- For the next class, show anonymous examples of good sentences and common errors.

UNIT REVIEW

Students can work in groups on this recap of the unit. For question **1**, encourage students to use the target words when appropriate. For questions **2** and **3**, encourage them to check the relevant pages of the unit for answers.

- Allow students time to answer the three questions in groups.
- Ask each group to share its answer for question **1**.

DON'T GIVE UP!

ACADEMIC TRACK

Psychology / Education

ACADEMIC SKILLS

READING	Identifying main ideas of paragraphs
WRITING	Ordering ideas
GRAMMAR	Using *want* and *need*
CRITICAL THINKING	Identifying evidence

UNIT OVERVIEW

The theme of this unit is perseverance and how it helps people succeed. From the oldest elementary school student in the world to young girls overcoming the odds in Afghanistan, these examples of perseverance show that even in very challenging circumstances, people can achieve their goals by not giving up.

- **READING 1:** At 84 years old, one Kenyan farmer overcame challenges to enroll as a first-grade student and learn to read.

- **VIDEO:** In a country where only three percent of women receive an education, one school is striving to change attitudes and create female leaders.

- **READING 2:** The results of a study on successful people show that they share these two traits: grit and self-control.

Students draw on what they've read and watched to write sentences about a learning goal. The unit prepares them for the writing task by introducing vocabulary related to learning, showing them how to use *want* and *need* in sentences, and teaching expressions for ordering ideas. It then leads them through the stages of brainstorming, outlining, combining ideas, writing, revising, and editing.

THINK AND DISCUSS (page 21)

The photo is of teenager Ashima Shiraishi, a young American who has become one of the top competitive rock climbers in the world. In 2016, at age 15, she was named one of National Geographic's Adventurers of the Year. Many of her climbing videos can be found online.

- Have students study the picture, title, and captions.
- Discuss the photo as a class. Have students heard of Ashima Shiraishi? How did she get so good at climbing? What do they think the unit is about?
- Discuss the two questions as a class. Ask students to describe the school challenges they face and how they

deal with them. What are the challenges students in other parts of the world face?

THINK AND DISCUSS

Answers will vary. Possible answers:

1. With so many distractions available on TV and online, it's hard for students to stay focused on their studies and homework. / In some parts of the world, getting to school is a big challenge because students live far away. / Many students around the world need to balance school and helping to support their families.

2. School teaches us useful skills, such as reading, writing, problem solving, and critical thinking. It also teaches us to communicate and work in teams. We learn to manage challenging situations by juggling multiple assignments and deadlines.

EXPLORE THE THEME (pages 22–23)

The opening spread contains worldwide statistics about literacy and education. Literacy is explained in the first line of the paragraph. Ask students to think about how not being able to read and write could be challenging.

- Allow students time to study the spread and answer the questions individually.
- Check answers as a class. Elicit sample answers for exercise **A**, and ask students to imagine how their lives would be if they weren't able to attend school. How can countries improve literacy and school attendance rates?
- Elicit sample sentences from students for each of the blue words.

EXPLORE THE THEME

A 1. Literacy rates are higher in Europe, North America, Australia, and parts of Asia. They are lower in Africa and parts of South America.

2. Many children in North America, South America, Europe, Asia, and Australia go to school. Fewer children in Africa go to school.

3. In many cases, families are not able to pay for school, so children do not go.

B attend; primary; education (Note: *Elementary school* is another name for *primary school*; teachers *take attendance* when they call students' names at the beginning of class.)

Reading 1

30 MINS **PREPARING TO READ** *(page 24)*

A Building Vocabulary

The paragraph is about some of the serious challenges students around the world face. It contains four key vocabulary items that appear in the passage. Students should use contextual clues to deduce the meanings of the words. Remind students that identifying the parts of speech can help them understand new words better.

- Have students complete the task individually.
- Check answers as a class. Elicit sample sentences for each vocabulary item.

B Building Vocabulary

The three sentences each contain a vocabulary item from the passage. Students should use contextual clues to deduce the meanings of the words.

- Have students complete the task individually.
- Check answers as a class. Elicit sample sentences for each vocabulary item.

See Vocabulary Extension 2A on page 204 of the Student Book for additional practice with the prefixes in *and* im *(insecure, impossible).*

C Using Vocabulary

The questions prepare students for the reading passage. They get students to think about what their early years of school were like. Students should use the new vocabulary items while answering the two questions.

- Have students work in pairs to answer the questions.
- Discuss as a class. Elicit sample answers from students. Ask students how they felt when they started primary school.

D Brainstorming

Answers can be subjects (such as math or English), skills (such as reading or public speaking), or traits (such as confidence or honesty). Each idea should be brief. Offer students one or two examples.

- Have students complete the task individually.
- Discuss as a class. Elicit sample answers from students, and rank them in order of importance on the board. Ask whether students who can't go to primary school will be able to learn these lessons.

E Predicting

The title states that the man in the photo is a first grader, and the photo confirms that he is attending a primary school class. He is probably there to learn something normally taught to first graders. Ask students to also think about the topics already discussed in the unit. Students may conclude that he is there because he had difficulty going to school as a child or because he wants to learn how to read.

- Allow students time to read the title and study the photo.
- Have students discuss their answers in pairs.
- Discuss as a class. Revisit this question after completing the reading.

ANSWER KEY

PREPARING TO READ

A **1.** ordinary (Note: *Extraordinary*, covered in Unit 1, is an antonym of *ordinary*.)

2. believe

3. decide

4. government

B **1.** a; **2.** b; **3.** a

C Answers will vary. Possible answers:

1. The primary school I attended was very small. I come from a village in a mountainous area, so there weren't many students. Each grade only had one class.

2. I am most motivated in my English class because I love Hollywood movies and I want to work there someday. / I am most motivated in my physics class. I would like to use science to help improve the environment.

D Answers will vary. Possible answers: reading, writing, algebra, basic math, science, chess, cooking, art, teamwork

E Answers will vary. Possible answers: He is attending class with the children because he wants to learn how to read. / I think the man is attending the class as an adult because he couldn't go to school as a child.

🎧 **3** Have students read the passage individually, or play the audio and have students read along.

OVERVIEW OF THE READING

The passage is about Kimani Maruge, a Kenyan farmer who decided to attend primary school at the age of 84. As a child, Maruge grew up poor and was unable to attend primary school. As an 84-year-old adult, he had to overcome several obstacles before a primary school would accept him. Maruge eventually succeeded and continued studying until the seventh grade. He spent his final years learning and teaching other elderly Kenyans to read. In 2005, Maruge spoke before the United Nations about the importance of free primary education. In 2010, his story was made into a movie, which inspired many to follow his example.

Online search terms: Kimani Maruge, The First Grader

 ## UNDERSTANDING THE READING
(page 27)

A Understanding Main Ideas

Students should select the option that best summarizes what the passage says about Maruge.
- Have students complete the task individually.
- Check answers as a class. Ask students where they found the answers.

B Understanding Details

Students fill in the blanks to complete phrases about events from Maruge's life. The events are deliberately not in order because students will have to rearrange them in the next exercise.
- Have students complete the exercise individually.
- Check answers as a class. Ask students where they found their answers.

C Sequencing

Students complete the timeline with the events from exercise **B**. The passage does not give dates for some of the events, so students will have to infer their order.
- Have students complete the task in pairs.
- Check answers as a class. Ask students where they found their answers.

D Critical Thinking: Identifying Evidence

The *Critical Thinking* box explains that as readers, we should pay attention to evidence that supports our ideas or assumptions. For the exercise, students should list adjectives that they think describe Maruge and look for evidence in the passage to support their opinions. Tell students that they should change their adjectives if there is no evidence to support them.
- Allow students time to complete the task individually.
- Have them discuss their answers in pairs.
- Discuss as a class. Elicit sample answers and ask whether anyone disagrees. Try to elicit opposing opinions, and encourage a debate.

ANSWER KEY

UNDERSTANDING THE READING

A   c (See Paragraphs B and C: Maruge faced difficulty attending primary school both as a child and as an adult.)

B a. farmer (See Paragraph B: When Maruge grew up, he worked as a farmer.)

b. movie (See Paragraph G: The 2010 movie *The First Grader...*)

c. war (See Paragraph B: He fought against the British in the 1950s.)

d. taught (See Paragraph E: Maruge taught residents to read and write.)

e. principal (See Paragraph C: A school principal helped Maruge stay in school.)

f. spoke (See Paragraph F: In 2005, Maruge gave a speech at the United Nations in New York City.)

g. refugee camp (See Paragraph E: Maruge moved to a refugee camp but continued to attend school.)

C   *From left to right:* **a** (See Paragraph B: Maruge became a farmer before fighting the British.); **c; e** (See Paragraph C: The principal helped Maruge shortly after 2003, when education was made free.); **f; g; d** (See Paragraph E: He taught residents at a home for the elderly in 2008, after he had moved to a refugee camp earlier that year.); **b** (Note: Specific dates are given for **b, c, f,** and **g**; but students need to infer dates for **a, d,** and **e**.)

D   Answers will vary. Possible answers: Hardworking. He was a farmer and a soldier, and both are difficult jobs. / Strong-willed. Continued to study even when many parents didn't want him in their children's class. / Determined. Didn't stop studying, even when he was forced to move to a refugee camp.

DEVELOPING READING SKILLS *(page 28)*

Reading Skill: Identifying Main Ideas of Paragraphs

The *Reading Skill* box explains that a paragraph usually has one main idea, with the rest of the information in the paragraph supporting the main idea. The main idea is described in the topic sentence, which is usually at the beginning or end of a paragraph.

A Identifying Main Ideas

Students are asked to select the statement that best describes the main idea of the paragraph and then identify the sentence in the paragraph that states this main idea.

- Allow students time to complete the exercise.
- Check answers as a class.

B Identifying Main Ideas

This exercise relates to Reading 1. Students go back to the passage to identify the main idea of four paragraphs.

- Allow students time to complete the task individually.
- Check answers as a class. Ask students for the topic sentence for each paragraph.

ANSWER KEY

DEVELOPING READING SKILLS

A 2. c;   3. c

B 1. G (Explanation: *Many older Kenyans decided to start school after seeing* The First Grader.)

  2. C (Explanation: *However, it wasn't always easy for him to attend school.*)

  3. A (Explanation: *However, Kimani Maruge was not an ordinary first grader.*)

  4. E (Explanation: *However, even during those difficult times, he continued to go to school.*)

Video

VIEWING: A SCHOOL FOR CHANGE *(pages 29–30)*

Overview of the Video

A school in Afghanistan is challenging traditional values by educating a new group of leaders: girls. Education for girls in Afghanistan is rare, but one school is working to change that. The groundbreaking School of Leadership of Afghanistan (SOLA) was founded by Shabana Basij-Rasikh, an Afghan woman who studied both locally and in the United States where she earned her college degree. Basij-Rasikh hopes to inspire a new generation of Afghan girls to study and rise to leadership positions, and through the education provided at SOLA, she believes that she is not only changing the girls, but also the traditional mindsets of their families and their communities.

Online search terms: School of Leadership Afghanistan, Shabana Basij-Rasikh

BEFORE VIEWING

A Predicting

The title states that this is a school setting. According to the caption, the three girls are students. They are decorating head scarfs, which are typically worn by women. There are notably no boys in the photo. These observations suggest that this may be a girls-only school. Students may also notice the name of the school written on the wall and draw conclusions from it.

- Allow some time for students to study the title, photo, and caption.
- Discuss as a class. Ask students whether they have ever heard of a school for leadership. What do they think is the objective of such a school?

B Learning About the Topic

The paragraph prepares students for the video by familiarizing them with the difficulties Afghan girls face in getting an education.

- Have students complete the exercise individually.
- Check answers as a class. Elicit sample answers from students. Have students refer to the infographic on pages 22–23. Based on the statistics in the paragraph, how does Afghanistan compare with the rest of the world? How can people and the government improve education for Afghan girls?

C Vocabulary in Context

This exercise introduces students to some of the key words used in the video. The paragraph also provides more information about why it is hard for girls to get an education in Afghanistan.
- Have students complete the exercise individually.
- Check answers as a class. Elicit sample sentences for each word.

BEFORE VIEWING

A Answers will vary. Possible answers: I think this is a school for girls in a place where girls don't normally go to school. / I think the school is training its students to one day take on leadership roles.

B 1. Families don't believe girls should go to school. / Families cannot afford school. / It's often not safe for girls to attend.

2. b (Explanation: Thirty-eight percent of children are not able to go to school.)

C 1. sibling

2. minority (Note: The opposite of *minority* is *majority*.)

3. priority (Note: While a *priority* or a *high priority* is something that is of great importance, a *low priority* is not very important.)

WHILE VIEWING

A ▶ Understanding Main Ideas

Have students read the items before you play the video.
- Have them complete the task while the video is playing.
- Check answers as a class. Explain that while all the options are probably benefits of an education at SOLA, the video only mentions some of them specifically.

B ▶ Understanding Details

Have students read the questions and write any answers they recall from the first viewing before playing the video a second time.
- Play the video again. Have students complete the task while the video is playing.
- Check answers as a class. Ask students where they found the answers.

WHILE VIEWING

A 1, 3, 4, 6

B 1. F; **2.** F; **3.** T; **4.** T

AFTER VIEWING

A Reacting to the Video

Students are asked in question **1** to think about what it means to be a global citizen. Are their schools similar to SOLA? Question **2** is a synthesizing exercise that requires students to draw on information from two sources to formulate their answers.
- Allow students time to answer the questions in pairs.
- Discuss as a class. For question **2**, draw a Venn diagram on the board to aid in discussion of the similarities and a few differences between Maruge and Basij-Rasikh.

B Critical Thinking: Evaluating

Students are asked to evaluate a statement made by Basij-Rasikh in the video. Encourage students to think beyond what has been covered in the unit so far.
- Allow students time to answer the questions in pairs or small groups.
- Discuss as a class. Elicit sample answers from students. Prompt students with hints and examples, if necessary.

AFTER VIEWING

A Answers will vary. Possible answers:

1. A global citizen is someone who knows a lot about what happens in the rest of the world. / who understands and appreciates cultural differences around the world. / who travels a lot and who can communicate well with people from different countries.

2. Both Maruge and Basij-Rasikh overcame many challenges to go to school. They were able to inspire and teach others, and both became role models.

B Answers will vary. Possible answers:

her family: She can get a job and help support her family financially.

her community: Women will be able to start businesses and provide jobs for others. / Women can become teachers who will help others receive education.

the world: There will be more women in leadership positions. / Women will be able to speak up about social issues or problems that women around the world face. / Fewer people will be unemployed, and global poverty will be reduced.

Reading 2

PREPARING TO READ (page 31)

A Building Vocabulary

The paragraph is about how people can improve their vocabularies by staying focused and not giving up. These are characteristics of *grit*, the subject of the reading passage. It contains four key vocabulary items that appear in the passage. Students should use contextual clues to deduce the meanings of the words.

- Have students work individually to complete the exercise.
- Check answers as a class. Elicit sample sentences for each vocabulary item. Go over the techniques described in the paragraph. Remind students to keep a vocabulary notebook and follow the tips in the passage, if they have not started doing this in Unit 1.

B Building Vocabulary

Students should first use dictionaries to check the definitions of the words in blue before using the words to complete the four sentences.

- Have students complete the exercise individually.
- Check answers as a class. Elicit example sentences for each vocabulary item.

See Vocabulary Extension 2B on page 204 of the Student Book for additional practice with collocations of the adverb up (give up, make up).

C Using Vocabulary

Students should use the new vocabulary items while discussing the two questions.

- Have students discuss the answers in pairs.
- Check answers as a class. Elicit sample answers from students.

D Predicting

The first paragraph states the main question and observations driving Duckworth's research. Although it provides no answer or explanation, the passage's title and the heading of the sidebar do. Point students to these, and remind them of the unit's theme.

- Allow students time to read the first paragraph.
- Discuss as a class. Elicit sample answers from students. Revisit this question after completing the reading.

ANSWER KEY

PREPARING TO READ

A 1. skill

2. similar (Note: Emphasize the word *almost* in the definition.)

3. give up (Note: The unit title is *Don't Give Up!* To *give up* is to surrender or to stop doing something because you believe you're not able to.)

4. record (Note: The verb *record* in the paragraph applies to written words, but it is also frequently applied to audio and video data.)

B 1. programs

2. advice (Note: The verb form of the noun *advice* is *advise*.)

3. solve

4. develop

C Answers will vary. Possible answers:

1. My father's cooking skills are excellent. / My sister has amazing drawing skills.

2. My father developed his cooking skills by studying cookbooks and learning new recipes. / My sister developed her drawing skills by taking art lessons and practicing every day.

D Answers will vary. Possible answers:

The smarter kids didn't try as hard as the kids with the lower IQs. / The kids with the lower IQs studied and practiced more, and so they were better at taking tests. / The smarter kids felt they had less to learn, so they paid less attention in class.

🎧 **4** Have students read the passage individually, or play the audio and have students read along.

OVERVIEW OF THE READING

Psychologist Angela Lee Duckworth realized when she was a teacher that the smartest kids were often not the most successful. She began researching why this was often the case and came to the conclusion that intelligence does not determine success. Instead, these two factors do: grit and self-control. When people persevere and work toward long-term goals, they tend to succeed. The passage is based on Duckworth's TED Talk: *The Key to Success? Grit.*

Online search terms: Angela Duckworth, The Key to Success? Grit

(page 34)

A Understanding Purpose

Students must match paragraphs from the reading to their purposes. Explain that the purpose of a paragraph is tied very closely to its main idea. Why is the author trying to get this main idea across?

- Allow students time to complete the activity individually. Encourage them to reread each paragraph, if necessary.
- Check answers as a class. Ask students where they found their answers.

B Summarizing

The summary is of the results of Duckworth's study, not of the whole passage. Answers can be found in Paragraphs C and D. Stress that students should answer in their own words.

- Allow students time to complete the activity individually.
- Check answers as a class. Elicit sample answers from students. Explain that summarizing in one's own words aids in comprehension and is a great way to prepare for tests and projects.

C Categorizing

This exercise tests students' understanding of the concepts of *grit* and *self-control*.

- Have students complete the exercise individually.
- Check answers as a class. Have students explain their answers. Ask students to describe ways they have demonstrated grit and self-control in their own lives.

D Critical Thinking: Inferring

Students need to understand the main idea of the passage to select the advice Duckworth would most likely give.

- Have students answer the question individually.
- Check answers as a class. Ask students how they arrived at their answers. Have them explain why the other two options are incorrect.

E Critical Thinking: Applying

Students examine how information in the reading passage relates to their own lives by drawing parallels with people they know. Go over the example with students. Complete sentences are not necessary.

- Allow students time to complete the chart individually.
- Have them check answers in pairs.
- Discuss as a class. Ask students for sample answers.

UNDERSTANDING THE READING

A **1.** b (Explanation: …*Angela Duckworth made a surprising discovery*)

    2. c (Explanation: *She began to research people in a variety of fields…*)

    3. a (Explanation: *From her research, Duckworth realized that…*)

    4. d (Explanation: *To be successful at what you do, Duckworth has this advice…*)

B Answers will vary. Possible answers:

    People with grit are able to <u>work hard and persevere</u>, while people with self-control <u>are able to finish what they are doing without getting distracted / sacrifice small short-term rewards for bigger long-term objectives</u>.

C **1.** S (Explanation: The speaker avoided a distraction.)

    2. G (Explanation: The speaker persevered despite multiple failures.)

    3. G (Explanation: The speaker persisted until his or her parents were convinced.)

    4. S (Explanation: The speaker avoided spending unnecessarily to save for the future.)

D b (See Paragraph F: *if you create a vision for yourself and stick with it,…*)

E Answers will vary. Possible answers: My cousin: hardworking; graduated with honors even though she had to work long hours while studying to pay her fees. / My brother: self-control; saved everything he earned for three years so he could afford a trip around the world.

Writing

OVERVIEW

In this section, students learn to write sentences about things that people *want* and *need*, and order their ideas sequentially. The lesson starts by teaching students when and how to use *want* and *need* in sentences. It then teaches students how to link their sentences in a step-by-step order, using words like *first*, *then*, and *finally*. In the *Writing Task*, students apply these lessons by writing sentences about a learning goal they *want* to accomplish and what they *need* to do to achieve it. Students improve their sentences by linking them together to show order. They then check for common mistakes related to the use of *want* or *need* in their sentences.

 30 MINS EXPLORING WRITTEN ENGLISH
(pages 35–37)

A Noticing

While completing this exercise, students should notice that the word *want* describes what somebody *would like* to do and that the word *need* describes what somebody *must* do. This exercise is to be done before going over the information in the *Language for Writing* box.

- Have students complete the exercise individually.
- Check answers as a class. Ask students how they arrived at their answers.

Language for Writing: Using *want* and *need*

The *Language for Writing* box explains how to use the word *want* for things we wish for and the word *need* for things we must do or can't do without. Both are used before *to* + base verb or a noun phrase. After going through the box, have students revisit the answers in **A** and underline the words expressing *want* and *need*.

B Language for Writing

Students apply what they learned in the box to unscramble the words and correctly form sentences describing *wants* and *needs*.

- Allow students time to complete the activity individually.
- Have them check answers in pairs.
- Discuss answers as a class.

C Language for Writing

Students practice when to use *want* and when to use *need* in this exercise by circling the correct option in each sentence. Explain that *need* can describe something essential, such as water or shelter, or something that must

be done to achieve something else. (Example: We *need* flour to bake a cake.)

- Have students complete the exercise individually.
- Check answers as a class. Have students explain their answers. Point out that people sometimes say they *need* something when they really just *want* it very badly. ("I *need* to have a slice of that cake. It looks so delicious!")

D Language for Writing

Students practice making simple sentences about their *wants* and *needs*. Have students think about their plans for the next few years and list two *wants* and two *needs* in the chart, using brief points. Next, have students pair up and take turns sharing their lists before they write their answers in complete sentences. Go over the examples with students before beginning the exercise.

- Have students complete the chart individually.
- Have students pair up and ask each other questions.
- Have them write their complete sentences individually.
- Discuss as a class. Elicit sample sentences. Ask if one person's *need* can be another person's *want* and vice versa.

Writing Skill: Ordering Ideas

The *Writing Skill* box introduces sequencing expressions such as *first, second, next, then,* and *finally*. It mentions two ways that ideas can be organized using expressions like these: as steps in a process or in order of importance. For the exercises, students will focus mainly on the former.

E Writing Skill

Students need to number the steps to achieve the specified goal correctly.
- Have students complete the task individually.
- Check answers as a class.

F Writing Skill

Students are expected to use the tips and sequencing expressions in the *Writing Skill* box to link the sentences in **E** in the correct order and draft a plan to apply to a college.
- Have students complete the task individually. Provide assistance as needed.
- Have them check their answers in pairs.
- Discuss as a class. Elicit sample sentences from students. Ask for different ways to introduce each step.

ANSWER KEY

WRITING SKILL

E **a.** 5

    b. 1

    c. 2

    d. 4

    e. 3

F Answers will vary. Possible answer:

    First, I need to decide what I want to study.

    Second, I need to do some online research and identify some colleges…

    Next, I need to find out as much as I can about the colleges…

    Then, after learning more about my choices, I need to decide…

    Finally, I need to complete and submit my applications.

    (Note: The meanings of *first* and *firstly* are the same. The same is true for *second* and *secondly*, and so on. Students can use either style, but they should be consistent. Avoid *Firstly* followed by *Second*, or *First* followed by *Secondly*.)

 WRITING TASK *(page 38)*

A Brainstorming

Remind students that brainstorming is a useful first step for gathering ideas before writing. Read the *Goal* box aloud so students are familiar with the writing task before brainstorming. Students should think of two learning goals and what they will need to do to achieve each goal. Provide students with an example. Ideas should be briefly worded, and steps need not be listed in order.
- Allow students time to complete the task individually.
- Have students share their ideas in pairs and give each other feedback.

B Planning

Students will need to select the learning goal that they prefer and single out the three most important things they need to do to achieve the goal. They should then organize their information in their outlines, listing their steps in a logical order. Remind students that complete sentences are not necessary. It is more important to focus on organizing their information.
- Allow students time to complete their outlines individually. Provide assistance as needed.

C First Draft

Have students write first drafts of their sentences based on their outlines.
- Allow students time to complete the task individually. Provide assistance as needed. Refrain from error correction at this point.

ANSWER KEY

WRITING TASK

A Answers will vary. Possible answers:

    Things I want to learn: gardening / how to speak Korean / how to cook Thai food

    Places where I want to learn: a community center / the Internet / a cooking class in Thailand

    Things I need to do or get: gardening tools / search the Internet for Korean language tutorials / buy plane tickets and book a hotel room

B Answers will vary. Possible answer:

    I want to <u>visit Thailand and learn how to cook traditional Thai food</u>.

    I need to <u>search the Internet for a good cooking course in Thailand</u>.

    I need to <u>buy plane tickets</u>.

    I need to <u>book a hotel room for two weeks</u>.

    I need to <u>continue practicing when I return by preparing Thai meals for my friends</u>.

REVISING PRACTICE   (page 39)

The *Revising Practice* box contains an exercise that demonstrates several ways students can improve their first drafts.

- Allow students time to analyze the two drafts and complete the exercise.
- Check answers as a class. Ask students to identify each change and explain how it makes the revised draft stronger.

D Revised Draft

Students should apply the revision techniques used in the *Revising Practice* box to their own drafts, where applicable.

- Explain to students that they will be using the questions as a guide for checking and improving their drafts.
- As a class, go over the questions carefully to make sure students understand them.
- Allow students time to revise their sentences.

EDITING PRACTICE

The *Editing Practice* box trains students to spot and correct common errors related to the use of *want* and *need* in sentences. As a class, go over the information in the box carefully to make sure students understand what to look out for.

- Allow students time to complete the exercise individually.
- Check answers as a class by asking students to read their corrected sentences aloud and explain the errors.

E Final Draft

Have students apply the skills taught in *Editing Practice* to their own revised drafts and check for any other errors.

- Allow students time to work individually on editing their drafts.
- Walk around and monitor students as they work. Provide assistance as needed.
- Collect their work once they have completed it.
- For the next class, show anonymous examples of good sentences and common errors.

UNIT REVIEW

Students can work in groups on this recap of the unit. For question **1**, encourage students to use the target words when appropriate. For questions **2** and **3**, encourage them to check the relevant pages of the unit for answers.

- Allow students time to answer the three questions in groups. For question **1**, ask students how they plan to use this advice in the future.
- Ask each group to present its answer for question **1**.

ANSWER KEY

REVISING PRACTICE

a, d, b, c, c

EDITING PRACTICE

1. You need <u>to get</u> a passport before you can study in Canada.

2. Students <u>need</u> to take an entrance exam if they want to apply to college.

3. The school wants <u>to build</u> a new library next year.

4. Maruge went to primary school because he wanted <u>to learn</u> to read.

5. I need <u>to write</u> an essay for my college application.

WHY WE BUY

ACADEMIC TRACK

Business / Marketing

ACADEMIC SKILLS

READING	Identifying supporting ideas
WRITING	Writing paragraphs and topic sentences
GRAMMAR	Connecting ideas
CRITICAL THINKING	Relating ideas

UNIT OVERVIEW

The unit explores the psychology behind making choices, especially regarding shopping. Brands and advertisements persuade us to make buying decisions every day. In this unit, we learn about some of the strategies used and why they work.

- **READING 1:** The way supermarkets are laid out is strategically designed to make us want to buy more.

- **VIDEO:** A quick look is all it takes for our brains to recognize key facial features and decide who we can trust.

- **READING 2:** Advertisers use priming to influence our attitudes, speed up our decision-making, and persuade us.

Students draw on what they've read and watched to write a full paragraph analyzing an advertisement. The unit prepares them by introducing vocabulary to use in talking about advertisements and persuasion and by describing some of the techniques used by advertisers. It teaches students how to identify and use supporting ideas that elaborate on the main idea of a paragraph and introduces language for connecting ideas that are non-sequential. Lastly, it helps students move on from writing sentences to writing paragraphs by explaining how to build a paragraph around a topic sentence.

THINK AND DISCUSS (page 41)

The photograph is of a crowded shopping district in Tokyo, with shoppers surrounded by signs and advertising. The title hints that the unit is about shopping, and the caption narrows this down further by drawing attention to the advertisements.

- Have students study the picture, title, and caption.

- Discuss the photo as a class. How do students feel about the bright lights? What do they think the signs are about?

- Discuss the questions as a class. For question **1**, elicit examples from as many different forms of media as possible, such as print, radio, TV, and the Internet. For question **2**, students will read related statistics in *Explore the Theme*.

ANSWER KEY

THINK AND DISCUSS

Answers will vary. Possible answers:

1. Most of the advertisements I see are on social media. They are usually for clothes and cosmetics. / I see a lot of ads for cameras because I like to read photography magazines.

2. Maybe 100? It's hard to say. I don't really pay attention to advertisements! (Note: Students will learn in *Explore the Theme* that the average adult in the United States sees a few hundred ads per day.)

EXPLORE THE THEME (pages 42–43)

The opening spread provides information and statistics about advertising in the United States. Mainly, it compares the popularity and effectiveness of TV and online ads.

- Allow students time to study the spread and answer the questions individually.

- Check answers as a class. Ask students why they think online ads have overtaken TV ads in popularity. Do the statistics reflect their own viewing and spending habits?

- Elicit sample sentences from students for each of the blue words.

ANSWER KEY

EXPLORE THE THEME

A 1. Most companies today prefer to use online ads instead of TV ads.

   2. TV ads are much more effective than social media ads in getting people to spend their money. Thirty-seven percent of people make buying decisions after watching TV ads. The number is only seven percent for ads on social media.

B percent; product; trust (Note: *Percent* is often represented by the percent symbol: %.)

Reading 1

PREPARING TO READ *(page 44)*

A Building Vocabulary

The paragraph is about the history and growth of online shopping. It contains four key vocabulary items that appear in the passage. Students should use contextual clues to deduce the meanings of the words.

- Have students work individually to complete the exercise.
- Check answers as a class. Elicit sample sentences for each vocabulary item.

B Building Vocabulary

The sentences in the box contain three key vocabulary items that appear in the reading passage. Students should use contextual clues to deduce the meanings of the words.

- Have students work individually to complete the exercise.
- Check answers as a class. Elicit sample sentences for each vocabulary item.

See Vocabulary Extension 3A on page 205 of the Student Book for additional practice with common collocations of the noun control *(lose control, take control).*

C Using Vocabulary

Students should use the new vocabulary items while discussing the questions about their shopping habits.

- Have students work in pairs to answer the questions.
- Check answers as a class. Elicit sample answers from students.

D Predicting

This prediction exercise does *not* require students to skim through parts of the passage. However, the title and photo caption do suggest that items are not placed randomly in a supermarket. Instead, supermarkets place items strategically so that people buy more. Students should guess the logic behind some of the item locations.

- Have students answer the question in pairs.
- Discuss as a class. Revisit this question after completing the reading.

PREPARING TO READ

A 1. attractive
   2. instead of
   3. store
   4. avoid

B 1. c; **2.** a; **3.** b (Note: For question **2**, compare paying in *cash* with paying by credit card.)

C   Answers will vary. Possible answers:
   1. I pay with cash when I buy only a few items that don't cost a lot. When I shop online, I use a credit card.
   2. I love buying clothes online, but I always buy shoes at the store so I can try them on first.

D   Answers will vary. Possible answer:
   I usually find milk together with other dairy products like cheese and yogurt. These are normally a little beyond the fruits and vegetables, which I always find close to the entrance. I think having healthy natural items like these near the entrance makes the supermarket look fresher and better. Candy is always near the exit. I get frustrated when I'm standing in line to pay, so I usually end up buying a snack to cheer myself up!

🎧 5   Have students read the passage individually, or play the audio and have students read along.

OVERVIEW OF THE READING

The passage is about how supermarkets are designed to persuade shoppers to buy more. From the locations of items in the store to the music that shoppers hear, every detail is crafted so that people buy more than they planned to. The passage describes the various tactics used and the logic behind them. It ends with some tips on how to avoid falling victim to the traps supermarkets set to make shoppers buy too much. The passage is based on the article "Surviving the Sneaky Psychology of Supermarkets," which appeared on National Geographic's food blog, *The Plate*.

Online search terms: supermarket psychology, Surviving the Sneaky Psychology of Supermarkets

UNDERSTANDING THE READING *(page 47)*

A Understanding Main Ideas

Students are asked to identify the main idea of the reading passage.

- Have students work individually to complete the activity.
- Check answers as a class. Ask students where they found the main idea.

B Understanding Details

Students use the details in the passage to label the supermarket diagram with the items in the box.

- Allow students time to complete the task individually.
- Have them check answers in pairs.
- Move on to exercise **C** before discussing the answers to exercise **B**.

C Understanding Purpose

Students must now identify the reasons why the items in exercise **B** are placed where they are.

- Have students complete the activity in pairs.
- Check answers for exercises **B** and **C** as a class. Ask students where they found their answers.

D Critical Thinking: Relating Ideas

The *Critical Thinking* box explains how to relate information to one's own experiences. Does the information match what students know or have experienced? Students should discuss the layouts of their local supermarkets before comparing them to the descriptions in the passage. Have students explain each similarity with a reason from the passage and each difference with a reason of their own. Lastly, have them decide whether each difference is an improvement.

- Allow students time to complete the task in pairs.
- Discuss answers as a class. Elicit sample answers. Students may live in the same area and visit the same supermarkets. If so, ask other students whether they agree, disagree, or have anything to add.

> **Ideas for… EXPANSION**
>
> To supplement exercise **D**, have students draw the layouts of their local supermarkets. Also, discuss which strategies have worked best on students in the past and why. Is it fair for supermarkets to secretly influence buying habits this way? Will knowing about these techniques change students' buying habits?

UNDERSTANDING THE READING

A   b (See Paragraph A)

B 1. fruit and vegetables (See Paragraph B: These are near the entrance.)

2. expensive cereal (See Paragraph C: Expensive items are at eye level.)

3. cheap cereal (See Paragraph C: Cheaper items are on lower shelves.)

4. milk (See Paragraph C: Popular items, such as milk and eggs, are at the back.)

5. cash registers (See Paragraph C: These are by the exit.)

C 1. d (See Paragraph C)

2. e (See Paragraph C)

3. c (See Paragraph C)

4. b (See Paragraph C)

5. a (See Paragraph B)

D   Answers will vary. Possible answer: My local supermarket almost matches the description in the passage, except that meats are at the back and milk is near the front next to the vegetables, together with other dairy products such as yogurt and cheese. This is a much better arrangement. The smell of meat is strong, and I don't like it being the first thing I notice. Also, dairy products are healthy and delicious. When I see a good dairy selection, I can't help myself. I just have to take a look!

 **DEVELOPING READING SKILLS** *(page 48)*

Reading Skill: Identifying Supporting Ideas

The *Reading Skill* box explains how *examples* and *reasons* are used to support the main idea of a paragraph, which is expressed in its topic sentence. Examples explain *what* and *how*, while reasons explain *why*. Note that examples and reasons are only two types of supporting ideas. Students will be focusing on these two types of supporting ideas in this unit's writing task.

A Identifying Supporting Ideas

Students should read the paragraph and spot the examples and the reasons in it. Each example in the paragraph is followed by a corresponding reason.

- Allow students time to complete the task individually.
- Check answers as a class. Ask students how they arrived at their answers.

B Categorizing

Main ideas define the content of a paragraph, while supporting ideas expand on a main idea. Students need to locate the sentences in the reading passage and label them accordingly.

- Have students complete the task individually.
- Have them check answers in pairs.
- Discuss as a class. Ask students how they arrived at their answers.

ANSWER KEY

DEVELOPING READING SKILLS

A Examples:

1. One way is placing products for children on lower shelves.
2. Another strategy is giving out free food samples.
3. Supermarkets also place candy and other cheap items at the registers.

Reasons:

1. This makes it easier for children to see and then ask their parents to buy something.
2. Seeing, tasting, and smelling food can make people feel hungry and want to buy it.
3. . . . customers might buy a snack while they wait in line.

(Note: The first sentence is the topic sentence. All *examples* and *reasons* elaborate on this topic sentence. The *examples* describe supermarket strategies, while the *reasons* explain why these strategies exist.)

B 1. M (See Paragraph A)
2. S (See Paragraph C)
3. M (see Paragraph D)
4. S (see Paragraph D)

Video

VIEWING: WHO DO YOU TRUST?
(pages 49–50)

Overview of the Video

According to research, our brains instantly find some faces more trustworthy than others. In the video, a TV show host re-creates an experiment originally performed by psychologist Alex Todorov. In the original experiment, Todorov discovered that winners of political elections, as opposed to their opponents, tend to have faces that people trust. He then identifies and explains these features. The video is an excerpt from the National Geographic Channel television show *Brain Games*.

Online search terms: Alexander Todorov, persuasive face, Face Value: The Irresistible Influence of First Impressions

BEFORE VIEWING

A Analyzing

The photos show four different faces. Students are asked to choose the face that instinctively seems the most trustworthy to them.

- Allow some time for students to study the photos.
- Have students discuss their first impressions with a partner.
- Discuss as a class. Ask students to give reasons for their first impressions. Take a class poll to see which face students find most trustworthy.

B Learning About the Topic

The paragraph prepares students for the video by giving them background information about Todorov's research, which is further explained in the video. Students should infer which of the statements agree with the findings of Todorov's research. Inform students that there is more than one correct answer.

- Have students complete the activity individually.
- Check answers as a class. Ask students why the incorrect statement is wrong.

C Vocabulary in Context

This exercise introduces students to some of the key words used in the video. The paragraph also provides more information about how people often form quick impressions of others.

- Have students complete the task individually.
- Check answers as a class. Elicit sample sentences for each word. Ask students to give examples of other kinds of *judgments* they make *in the blink of an eye*.

BEFORE VIEWING

A Answers will vary. Possible answer: I think the woman in the bottom right has the most persuasive face because of her wide smile.

B 2, 3 (Note: Option 1 is incorrect because the paragraph states that people are often influenced by other people's physical appearance, and does not mention anything about what they say.)

C **1.** trustworthy (Note: *Trustworthy* means worthy of, or deserving, trust.)

    2. judgment (Note: A *judgment* is an opinion that one forms after some consideration.)

    3. in the blink of an eye (Note: This expression refers to the split second it takes to blink.)

    4. candidate

    5. competent

WHILE VIEWING

A ▶ Understanding Main Ideas

Have students read the items before you play the video.
- Have them complete the task while the video is playing.
- Check answers as a class. Discuss why the other two options are wrong.

B ▶ Understanding Details

Have students read the questions and write any answers they recall from the first viewing before playing the video a second time. Students are asked to identify the results of Todorov's experiment.
- Have students complete the task while the video is playing.
- Check answers as a class. Discuss the findings described. Do students think that female faces appear more trustworthy?

WHILE VIEWING

A b

B **1.** b; **2.** a; **3.** a (Explanation: Option b is incorrect because the video does not mention anything about how to tell if someone is lying.)

AFTER VIEWING

A Reacting to the Video

Students are asked to think about their own first impressions of the three pairs of candidates the presenter showed at the start of the video. Replay the start of the video for students, if necessary. Did students guess the winners correctly? Which, if any, did they guess wrong? What made them choose the candidates they chose?
- Allow students time to answer the questions in pairs.
- Discuss as a class.
- For the second question, make a list on the board of the positive and negative impressions students had of each winning candidate. After that, ask students whether any of these impressions are correct.

> **Ideas for... EXPANSION**
>
> Have students perform an experiment similar to the one in the video. Ask students to work in groups to find a photo of a trustworthy face online or in a magazine. Then have each group present its photo to the class, and take a class vote. Which face looks most trustworthy? Why?

B Critical Thinking: Reflecting

Students are asked to share a personal story about a time that they made a quick judgment about another person.
- Allow students time to answer the questions in pairs.
- Discuss as a class. Elicit sample answers from students, and try to get stories in which snap judgments were useful and stories in which they were harmful. Ask for other examples that students may have heard of or read about somewhere.

AFTER VIEWING

A Answers will vary. Possible answers: I chose two out of three candidates correctly. I think I based my decision on their eyes. / I guessed two out of three candidates wrong. I'm not sure why. I know I'm not good at judging people by their appearance, and I try my best not to!

B Answers will vary. Possible answers: I didn't like my science teacher when I first met him. He had messy hair! But after taking his class for a while, I realized he was a great teacher and a nice person, and I even started to like his messy hair!

Reading 2

PREPARING TO READ *(page 51)*

A Building Vocabulary

In this exercise, the definitions of key words from the reading passage are provided. Students should use the definitions to help them complete the exercise.

- Have students complete the task individually.
- Check answers as a class. Elicit sample sentences for each vocabulary item.

See Vocabulary Extension 3B on page 205 of the Student Book for additional practice with common collocations of the adjective natural *(natural disaster, natural resources).*

B Using Vocabulary

Students should use the new vocabulary items while discussing the two questions.

- Have students work in pairs to answer the questions. Give students one or two examples of ads that are currently popular.
- Check answers as a class. Elicit sample answers from students.

C Predicting

The first paragraph asks how we decide to buy the things we buy, and the title of the passage provides us with a clue. The word *persuasion* suggests that we do not decide on our own what to buy, but that we are persuaded. Neither the title nor the paragraph states what is persuading us, but the photo should prompt students that it has something to do with advertising.

- Allow students time to skim through the first paragraph and the title.
- Discuss answers as a class. Revisit the question after completing the reading.

🎧 **6**   Have students read the passage individually, or play the audio and have students read along.

OVERVIEW OF THE READING

The reading describes priming and how it influences us to buy things. It suggests that sometimes we are not in control of our buying decisions and that advertisers use priming to dictate our preferences without us even noticing. Priming involves using cues to manipulate our attitudes and responses and to speed up our decision-making process. Color is an example of priming. Green, for example, makes products seem natural, so companies often use green packaging to persuade buyers that their products are healthy. Rhymes are also effective as a priming tool. Research shows that shoppers find rhyming ads to be more believable. The passage ends by getting us to reconsider who really makes our buying decisions for us.

Online search terms: *priming, advertising, Marketing to Your Brain*

40 MINS

A Summarizing

Students choose the right options to complete a summary of the passage's main idea.
• Have students complete the task individually.
• Check answers as a class. Ask students where they found their answers. Ask them to explain priming and to describe real-life examples they've encountered.

B Identifying Main Ideas

Students are asked to identify three main ideas that are discussed in the passage.
• Allow students time to complete the task individually.
• Check answers as a class. Ask students where they found their answers and why the incorrect options are *not* main ideas.

C Identifying Supporting Ideas

The three options are supporting ideas that expand on the main ideas from exercise **B**. Students should match each supporting idea to its corresponding main idea by filling in the blanks with the correct option numbers from exercise **B**.
• Allow students time to complete the task individually.
• Check answers as a class.

D Understanding Details

The exercise lists five different priming strategies. Numbers 1 to 4 are discussed in the passage. Number 5 is described in the *Advertising Strategies* box on page 52. Students should match the *Strategies* with their corresponding *Effects*, which are also the reasons why each strategy works.
• Allow students time to complete the task individually.
• Check answers as a class. Discuss which strategy is the most effective for different types of products.

E Critical Thinking: Reflecting

Students revisit the *Using Vocabulary* question on page 51 about interesting ads they recently noticed. They should identify the priming strategies used in the ad and reflect on how the priming strategies made the ad more memorable for them personally. Remind students to refer to the *Advertising Strategies* box for help.
• Allow students time to answer the questions individually.
• Have them discuss their answers in pairs.
• Discuss as a class. Elicit sample answers. Ask other students who have seen the ad to offer their opinions.

ANSWER KEY

UNDERSTANDING THE READING

A advertisers; quick (See Paragraph C)

B 2, 3, 5

C a. 5; **b.** 2; **c.** 3

D 1. d (See Paragraph D)
  2. c (See Paragraph D)
  3. b (See Paragraph E)
  4. a (See Paragraph F)
  5. e (See *Advertising Strategies* box)

E Answers will vary. Possible answers:

Techniques: Celebrity Power / Emotional Impact

Why it influenced you: The ad used my favorite rugby team, and I like the idea of drinking the same energy drink as they do. / An ostrich flying is silly, but I felt inspired when the ostrich proved everyone wrong and fulfilled its dream by taking flight.

Writing

See Grammar Reference on pages 219–223 of the Student Book for additional information on expressions for connecting ideas.

OVERVIEW

In this section, students progress from writing sentences, as they did in the previous two units, to writing a full paragraph. The lesson starts by teaching students new expressions for connecting ideas such as *In addition, Also,* and *Another* + noun. Students are then shown how to build a paragraph around a main idea using a topic sentence. In the *Writing Task*, students apply these lessons by writing a paragraph explaining why an ad is effective. Students begin the task by brainstorming for ideas and reasons. Then they select the best ones, add details, and organize them in an outline. Finally, students draft their paragraphs, improve their drafts, and correct common mistakes with connecting words and phrases.

EXPLORING WRITTEN ENGLISH *(pages 55–57)*

A Noticing

While completing the exercise, students should notice the difference between the circled and underlined words/phrases. This exercise is to be done before going over the information in the *Language for Writing* box.

• Have students complete the task individually.
• Check answers as a class.

Language for Writing: Connecting Ideas

The *Language for Writing* box gives examples of expressions that can be used to connect ideas. In Unit 2, students learned expressions for connecting sequential events (*First, Second, Next, Then, Finally*). Now they learn more general expressions for linking ideas that don't need to be listed in order. Highlight how commas should be used when these expressions appear at the start of a sentence.

B Language for Writing

Students practice using the connecting words and phrases in the box by listing three reasons they like to use a product. Ask students to write short answers for the first part of the exercise. When connecting their reasons in the second part of the exercise on page 56, students should write complete sentences.

• Allow students time to complete the activity individually.
• Have them share their answers in pairs.
• Discuss as a class. Elicit sample sentences from students.

Writing Skill: Writing Paragraphs and Topic Sentences

The *Writing Skill* box explains that a topic sentence describes the main idea of a paragraph. A paragraph has only one topic sentence. It is usually the first or last sentence of a paragraph. The rest of the paragraph supports or explains the topic sentence by providing supporting ideas such as examples, facts, or reasons.

C Identifying a Topic Sentence

Students need to identify what the supporting ideas in the paragraph have in common and select the best topic sentence. They should notice that each supporting idea refers to a specific store. Even though it is simply referred to as "the store" in the first sentence, students should notice in later sentences that the store in question is *SuperFoods*. The topic sentence should therefore mention *SuperFoods*.

• Allow students time to complete the task individually.
• Check answers as a class. Ask students why options a and b are not suitable topic sentences.

D Writing a Topic Sentence

Students need to read the paragraph and create a topic sentence for it. The supporting ideas in the paragraph describe three similar objectives: *buy less when you shop; avoid supermarket strategies; save money*. Students must create a topic sentence that ties these three points together.

- Allow students time to complete the task individually.
- Discuss answers as a class. Elicit sample topic sentences from students.

E Identifying Supporting Ideas

Good paragraphs do not contain sentences that are unrelated to the topic sentence. Students need to identify the two unrelated sentences in this paragraph. Make sure students know that the first sentence is the topic sentence before starting the exercise.
- Allow students time to complete the task individually.
- Check answers as a class. Have students explain why the sentences should be removed. Do they agree that the paragraph is better without the two sentences?

ANSWER KEY

WRITING SKILL

C c (Note: Item a is not suitable because it is a statement about all supermarkets, and not SuperFoods specifically; item b is a supporting idea in the form of an example.)

D Answers will vary. Possible answers:

There are a few ways that shoppers can avoid buying too much at the supermarket. / Customers can beat the strategies that supermarkets use to make them buy more.

E 3, 7 (Explanation: Both these sentences stray from the topic of color.)

WRITING TASK (page 58)

A Brainstorming

Remind students that brainstorming is a useful first step for gathering ideas before writing. Read the *Goal* box aloud so students are familiar with the writing task before brainstorming. Ensure students have access to print ads from magazines or newspapers before brainstorming. Students should consider several ads before selecting one. Have them analyze the selected ad, using questions **1** to **4** as a guide. Then they should list reasons why they think the selected ad is effective. Remind students to draw on what they've learned about advertising strategies in the unit. Ideas should be briefly worded. They need not be listed in any order.
- Allow students time to complete the task individually.
- Have students share their ideas in pairs and give each other feedback.

B Planning

Have each student choose the three best reasons and write a topic sentence that links them all. Point out that each reason is a supporting idea and that students need to add details to each supporting idea. Remind students that complete sentences are not necessary. It is more important to focus on organizing their information.
- Allow students time to complete their outlines individually. Provide assistance as needed.

C First Draft

Have students write first drafts of their paragraphs based on their outlines.
- Allow students time to complete the task individually. Provide assistance as needed. Refrain from error correction at this point.

ANSWER KEY

WRITING TASK

A Answers will vary. Possible answers:

Celebrity power / Vivid colors / A perfect family / A rhyming slogan / Emotional impact / A great soundtrack / Cool graphics / Funny script (Note: The priming techniques described in Reading 2 offer a useful list of reasons, but students should also try to come up with reasons of their own.)

B Answers will vary. Possible answers:

(Based on a dessert advertisement)

Topic sentence: This advertisement is effective because it uses clever techniques that make us feel positive about the product.

Supporting Idea 1: It suggests that we can have a perfect family.

Detail 1: Family is happily eating dessert together.

Supporting Idea 2: The ad uses colors effectively.

Detail 2: The red tablecloth makes us feel warm and happy; the green grass seems healthy and wholesome.

Supporting Idea 3: The slogan is catchy and memorable.

Detail 3: It rhymes, and it uses an attractive font.

REVISING PRACTICE   *(page 59)*

The *Revising Practice* box contains an exercise that demonstrates several ways students can improve their first drafts.

- Allow students time to analyze the two drafts and complete the exercise.
- Check answers as a class. Ask students to identify each change and explain how it makes the revised draft stronger.

D Revised Draft

Students should apply the revision techniques used in the *Revising Practice* box to their own drafts, where applicable.

- Explain to students that they will be using the questions as a guide for checking and improving their drafts.
- As a class, go over the questions carefully to make sure students understand them.
- Allow students time to revise their paragraphs.

EDITING PRACTICE

The *Editing Practice* box trains students to spot and correct common errors related to the use of expressions for connecting ideas. As a class, go over the information in the box carefully to make sure students understand what to look out for.

- Allow students time to complete the exercise individually.
- Check answers as a class by asking students to read their corrected sentences aloud and explain the errors.

ANSWER KEY

REVISING PRACTICE

    b, a, d, c

EDITING PRACTICE

1. <u>Firstly</u>, ads use emotional impact to make us believe that their product will affect our lives in a good way.

2. One technique is to place items in certain positions on the shelves. An additional <u>technique</u> is to use colors to affect the way we feel about a product.

3. <u>Furthermore</u>, some ads use celebrities.

4. <u>Finally</u>, ads should have clear messages that are easy to understand.

E Final Draft

Have students apply the skills taught in *Editing Practice* to their own revised drafts and check for any other errors.

- Allow students time to work individually on editing their drafts.
- Walk around and monitor students as they work. Provide assistance as needed.
- Collect their work once they have completed it.
- For the next class, show anonymous examples of good paragraphs and common errors.

UNIT REVIEW

Students can work in groups on this recap of the unit. For question **1**, encourage students to use the target words when appropriate. For questions **2** and **3**, encourage them to check the relevant pages of the unit for answers.

- Allow students time to answer the three questions in groups. For question **1**, ask students to decide which technique they like best and to use the technique to create an ad idea of their own.
- Ask each group to present its answer for question **1**. As a class, vote for the best ad idea.

GREEN LIVING

ACADEMIC TRACK
Environmental Science

ACADEMIC SKILLS
READING	Scanning for details
WRITING	Using supporting sentences
GRAMMAR	Stating problems and proposing solutions
CRITICAL THINKING	Analyzing problems and solutions

UNIT OVERVIEW

This unit encourages students to think more deeply about environmental issues, focusing primarily on the trash we produce. Students learn about activists and artists who work to raise awareness of the problems caused by trash and to promote recycling.

- **READING 1:** A giant island of trash floating in the Pacific Ocean is causing great environmental harm.

- **VIDEO:** An artist creates sculptures from trash and travels around the world with them to raise awareness of the world's trash problem.

- **READING 2:** An artist works with trash collectors to create a giant portrait made out of trash to highlight the important work done by these trash collectors.

Students draw on what they've read and watched to write a paragraph proposing possible solutions to an environmental problem. The unit prepares them for the writing task by introducing vocabulary that can be used to talk about environmental issues and language for discussing problems and solutions. The writing task builds on what students have learned in the last three units by teaching them how to effectively add supporting ideas and details to expand on main ideas.

THINK AND DISCUSS *(page 61)*

The photo shows a family lying on a beach surrounded by all the trash they produced in one week. The photo is meant to get students thinking about how much trash they produce and where it all goes.
- Have students study the picture, title, and caption.
- Discuss the photo as a class. Are students surprised by the amount of trash? Do they think that their families produce more trash or less?

- Discuss the two questions as a class. For question **1**, introduce useful phrases to start the discussion (*I think the photographer wants to show us that…*). For question **2**, ask who collects the trash and where they take it.

ANSWER KEY

THINK AND DISCUSS

Answers will vary. Possible answers:

1. I think the photographer is trying to show us trash is a bigger problem than most of us realize. I've never thought about what my trash would look like spread out like this!

2. In my neighborhood, trash collectors empty our bins into a huge truck every day. Most of our trash goes to a landfill, but some of it is incinerated (burned), too. We usually separate plastic, glass, aluminum, and paper items for recycling.

EXPLORE THE THEME *(pages 62–63)*

The opening spread describes three ideas for dealing with trash. The ideas focus on turning trash into something useful or reducing the amount produced in the first place.
- Allow students time to study the spread and complete the activities individually.
- Check answers as a class. Ask students which idea they like best and which is the most effective way of dealing with the problem of too much trash.
- Elicit sample sentences from students for each of the blue words.

ANSWER KEY

EXPLORE THE THEME

A 1. b; **2.** c; **3.** a

B collect; throw away; recycle (Note: The words *throw* and *away* are frequently separated by the direct object of a clause or sentence. For example, *Throw <u>it</u> away*.)

Ideas for… EXPANSION

As a class, brainstorm different words for *trash,* such as *garbage* and *rubbish*. Which types of trash can be recycled? Which are biodegradable (able to decompose over time)? Find out what the worst type of trash is: trash that's both non-biodegradable and non-recyclable.

Reading 1

PREPARING TO READ *(page 64)*

A Building Vocabulary

The paragraphs are about the problems caused by trash and how recycling helps. They contain seven key vocabulary items that appear in the passage. Students should use contextual clues to deduce the meanings of the words.

- Have students work individually to complete the exercise.
- Check answers as a class. Elicit sample sentences for each vocabulary item.

See Vocabulary Extension 4A on page 206 of the Student Book for additional practice with the prefix re- *(recycle, rethink).*

B Using Vocabulary

Students should use the new vocabulary items while discussing the two questions.

- Have students work in pairs to answer the questions.
- Discuss as a class. Elicit sample answers from students.

C Brainstorming

Students should think of as many everyday plastic items as possible. Give students one or two examples before they begin.

- Allow students time to create their lists in pairs.
- Discuss as a class. List ideas on the board, and single out the three items that are most frequently thrown away. Ask whether they can be recycled.

D Predicting

The title and first paragraph state clearly that the island is made of garbage floating in the Pacific Ocean. This photo of trash samples collected from the garbage patch suggests that the island contains a lot of plastic trash. Later paragraphs reveal that the island is created by ocean currents, which carry the plastic trash out into the middle of the ocean and prevent it from escaping.

- Allow students time to read the first paragraph and scan the title and captions.
- Have students discuss their answers in pairs.
- Discuss as a class. Revisit this activity after completing the reading.

Ideas for… EXPANSION

Have students search the Internet for images of the Great Pacific Garbage Patch. Some images show the plastic floating in the ocean, while others show the location and scale of the plastic "island" on maps. Other images show how the currents create a vortex (a spiral motion) that pulls things such as plastic trash into it.

ANSWER KEY

PREPARING TO READ

A 1. cause

   2. aware

   3. kill

   4. solution

   5. report

   6. float (Note: Things can float in a variety of ways and at various depths. For example, much of the garbage island is plastic floating just *beneath* the surface of the ocean,)

   7. clean up (Note: *Clean up* is often used in connection with environmental efforts. For example: *Many volunteers helped clean up the beach after the oil spill.*)

B   Answers will vary. Possible answers:

   1. Yes, it causes a lot of problems, especially at the beach. I live by the beach, and every morning, a lot of trash washes up on the beach from the ocean. We've tried cleaning it up a few times before, but it never stays clean for long.

   2. Last year, my high school helped clean up a river. We spent the morning picking up trash, and we recycled what we could. We even used some of the trash we found in school art projects.

C   Answers will vary. Possible answers: cups, plates, cutlery, chairs, food containers, toys, water bottles, plastic bags, cell phone casings

D   Answers will vary. Possible answer: The island is probably made up of pieces of plastic. They must have floated away from our beaches and drains to the middle of the ocean.

7 Have students read the passage individually, or play the audio and have students read along.

OVERVIEW OF THE READING

The passage describes a huge mass of plastic waste floating in the North Pacific Ocean. Spinning currents trap discarded plastic from Asia and North America, forming an island of garbage that is, according to some studies, already twice the size of the continental United States, and continues to grow every year. The plastic that makes up the island kills the animals that eat it and blocks sunlight from reaching plankton and algae—vital food sources for many ocean species. Some environmentalists are trying to raise awareness of the problem and seek solutions.

Online search terms: garbage island, garbage patch in Pacific Ocean, Cesar Harada

UNDERSTANDING THE READING *(page 67)*

A Understanding Main Ideas

Students are asked to identify the main idea of the passage.
- Have students complete the activity individually.
- Check answers as a class. Ask students why the other two options are wrong.

B Summarizing

Students complete a summary of the passage by choosing the correct options.
- Allow students time to complete the activity individually.
- Check answers as a class. Ask where students found the answers.

C Understanding a Process

Students fill in the blanks with words from the passage to complete the diagram. Paragraphs D and E describe a chain of events set in motion by the introduction of plastics to the ocean. The diagram illustrates this process, representing visually what the paragraphs are trying to say—that the events are not random or unrelated but that one harmful event triggers another.
- Allow students time to complete the task individually.
- Check answers as a class.

D Critical Thinking: Analyzing Problems and Solutions

The *Critical Thinking* box covers how to describe a problem and its solution. Explain that we usually describe the problem first because we need to understand the problem before a solution can be meaningful. Suggest that there are two ways to tackle a problem: by addressing the cause of it (prevent plastics from entering the ocean) or by addressing the result (clean up the plastic already in the ocean).
- Have students complete the first part of the activity individually.
- Allow students time to discuss the second part of the activity in pairs.
- Discuss as a class. For the second part of the activity, encourage students to think of solutions that address both the root cause and the result. Have them vote for the solutions they believe are most likely to work.

ANSWER KEY

UNDERSTANDING THE READING

A b (Note: Option a describes the main idea of Paragraph F, not the passage; the first half of option c is correct, but not the second, since we know the plastic comes from our trash.)

B 1. plastic
2. in a circle
3. attracts new objects
4. bigger
5. double

C 1. eat
2. sunlight
3. sea organisms
4. less food

D **Harada:** robot
Williams: recycling, aware

Answers will vary. Possible answers: Educate people more through the Internet, news, and social media. / Build machines to push the garbage to shore so that we can clean it up more easily. / Give people rewards for recycling plastic, so that we throw away less.

DEVELOPING READING SKILLS *(page 68)*

Reading Skill: Scanning for Details

Scanning is useful when we know what kind of information we are looking for. For example, if we need to find a date, we scan quickly for numbers that look like dates. Once we have found a number, we scan the surrounding information and decide whether we have the right information.

A Identifying

Inform students that they are not being asked to answer the questions. They should instead identify the type of information they need to scan for to answer the questions. Use question **1** as an example, if necessary.

- Allow students time to complete the exercise individually.
- Check answers as a class.

B Scanning for Details

Students should now answer the questions in **A** by scanning the paragraph in **B**. Students should look for the type of information required to answer each question (names, years, places, and numbers). Use question **1** as an example, if necessary.

- Allow students time to complete the exercise individually.
- Then have students read the passage slowly and check their own answers.
- Discuss as a class. Ask students where they found the answers. Did they spot other years, names, places, and numbers that were not the answers?

ANSWER KEY

DEVELOPING READING SKILLS

A **1.** name
   2. year
   3. place
   4. year
   5. number

B **1.** Charles Moore (a racing-boat captain)
   2. 1997
   3. California
   4. 2014
   5. more than 15 meters long

Video

VIEWING: TRASH PEOPLE
(pages 69–70)

Overview of the Video

German artist HA Schult uses trash found in a landfill to create sculptures of people. He displays his sculptures in different countries to make the point that garbage is a global problem. The video shows hundreds of his trash people assembled at well-known sites such as the Pyramids of Giza and the Great Wall of China. Schult believes that the children of today will one day solve our trash problem.

Online search terms: HA Schult, trash people sculptures

BEFORE VIEWING

A Predicting

The photo shows Schult's trash people lined up on the shores of a lake. This lake is at the foot of the Matterhorn, a famous mountain in Switzerland. The Matterhorn is a popular tourist destination. It is one of the well-known sites at which Schult placed his sculptures. Schult wants as many people as possible to see his sculptures and learn about the growing problem of trash.

- Have students study the title, photo, and caption in pairs.
- Discuss as a class. Why have so many "trash people" been assembled by a lake? Point out that the lake is at a famous tourist attraction, and ask students to look for it while watching the video.

B Learning About the Topic

The paragraph prepares students for the video by providing statistics that will help them better appreciate the scale of Earth's trash problem and the motivation behind Schult's work.

- Have students complete the task individually.
- Check answers as a class. Ask students whether they are surprised by the information.

C Vocabulary in Context

This exercise introduces students to some of the key words used in the video. The paragraph also provides more information about trash and how we usually process it.

- Have students complete the task individually.
- Check answers as a class. Elicit sample sentences for each word. Explain to students what a landfill is.

BEFORE VIEWING

A   Answers will vary. Possible answers: The sculptures look like they are made of trash. Perhaps they are made from trash that was found in the lake. / I think an artist made these to show that we have too much trash. It's quite shocking to see this much trash along these shores of a beautiful lake.

B   Answers will vary. Possible answers:

1. We produce about 1.3 billion tons of trash a year.

2. It is hard to find recycling bins in many parts of the world. It is much easier to simply throw things away. / Many people do not know how important it is to recycle.

3. Most of the world's trash comes from cities. As cities grow, the amount of trash produced grows as well.

C   1. sculpture (Note: *Solid*, as used in the definition, means three-dimensional.)

2. transform

3. garbage collector

4. set up

WHILE VIEWING

A ▶ Understanding Main Ideas

Have students read the items before you play the video.
- Have students complete the task while the video is playing.
- Check answers as a class.

B ▶ Understanding Details

Have students read the question and write any answers they recall from the first viewing before playing the video a second time. Ask students to pay close attention to the countries mentioned in the video because there are several.
- Have students complete the task while the video is playing.
- Check answers as a class.

> **Ideas for… EXPANSION**
>
> Discuss whether Schult's art succeeds in its mission to raise awareness. Why or why not? (Possible answers: It succeeds because the large number of statues on display helps us visualize how big the problem is. / It doesn't succeed. It's hard to feel that the trash used to make these displays poses a serious problem.)

WHILE VIEWING

A   1. a;   2. a

B   a, b, c, d, f, g

AFTER VIEWING

A Critical Thinking: Synthesizing

Students draw on information from *Reading 1* and the *Video* to complete the chart. Allow students to revisit the reading passage to find their answers.
- Allow students time to complete the task individually.
- Check answers as a class. Discuss whose work will likely have the biggest impact. How can the three people work together to achieve even better results? (For example, Harada's robots could supply Williams with materials for his clothing line.)

B Critical Thinking: Applying

Students apply the information in the video to their own lives by imagining Schult's art being on display in their hometowns. Students need to understand the goal of Schult's display and figure out how they can best achieve this goal.
- Allow students time to answer the questions in pairs.
- Discuss as a class. Elicit sample answers from students, and list ideas on the board. Have the class vote for the best location.
- Discuss how students think their city or town would react to the display. What can students do to make the display more effective? (For example, they could create posters explaining the message behind the art.)

AFTER VIEWING

A   deals with ocean trash: Harada, Williams

turns garbage into art: Schult

uses robot technology: Harada

turns trash into something you can use every day: Williams

B   Answers will vary. Possible answers: I think it would be best to put them along our main shopping street because many people will be able to see them. / I think it would be best to put them in our botanical gardens because the trash people will really stand out there against the beautiful scenery.

Reading 2

PREPARING TO READ *(page 71)*

30 MINS

A Building Vocabulary

In this exercise, the definitions of key vocabulary items from the reading passage are provided. Students should use the definitions to help them complete the exercise.

- Have students complete the task individually.
- Check answers as a class. Elicit sample sentences for each vocabulary item.

See Vocabulary Extensions 4B and 4C on page 206 of the Student Book for additional practice with antonyms (tall / short, reduce / increase).

B Using Vocabulary

Students should use the new vocabulary items while discussing the two questions. Have students search online for ideas, if needed.

- Have students work in pairs to answer the questions.
- Discuss as a class. Elicit sample answers from students.

C Predicting

The first paragraph states that Muniz's art is made from everyday objects. This suggests that he usually transforms old and unwanted things into works of art. The title, which specifically mentions recycling, confirms this. However, the last line of the paragraph suggests that Muniz does something unusual by using trash in his art. This is reinforced by the photo of the landfill, which is probably where Muniz sometimes collected materials for his art.

- Allow students time to skim through the first paragraph, title, photo, and caption.
- Have students discuss their answers in pairs.
- Discuss as a class. Revisit the question after completing the reading.

🎧 **8** Have students read the passage individually, or play the audio and have students read along.

OVERVIEW OF THE READING

The passage describes how artist Vik Muniz worked with garbage pickers, or *catadores*, at a landfill in Brazil to create a piece of art using garbage. He managed to sell a photograph of his art for $50,000, which he gave to the workers' organization. Through the project, Muniz wanted to improve the lives and raise the self-esteem of the catadores, who made a living by searching the landfill for materials such as aluminum cans and glass bottles to sell to recycling companies. Even though their work was difficult and dangerous and their wages were low, the catadores were proud of their jobs and the good they did for the environment.

Online search terms: Vik Muniz, Waste Land, Jardin Gramacho, catadores

UNDERSTANDING THE READING *(page 74)*

A Understanding Purpose

Students are asked to identify the purpose of various paragraphs from the passage.

- Allow students time to complete the activity individually.
- Check answers as a class. Ask students where they found the answers.

B Scanning for Details

Students should scan for the specific type of information each question is requesting. Tell students not to reread the passage, but to scan for key words and other clues for the answers.

- Have students complete the task individually.
- Check answers in pairs. Allow students to read the passage carefully to check their answers.
- Discuss as a class. Ask students where they found the answers and what words they used to scan quickly to find them.

C Sequencing

Students number the sentences in order, based on the events described in Paragraphs D, E, and F.

- Allow students time to complete the activity individually.
- Have students check their answers in pairs.
- Discuss as a class. Draw a timeline on the board, and ask students where each stage of the process should go.

D Critical Thinking: Inferring Meaning

To understand the quote, students should look for contextual clues. In Paragraph C, the speaker mentions that he is frequently asked by people whether recycling a single soda can makes any real difference environmentally. He answers with the quote, which is directed to not just one person, but to people in general. If many people care enough to recycle a single soda can, then one can of soda does make a difference.

- Allow students time to answer the question in pairs.
- Discuss as a class. Ask students why the other two options are wrong. Do students agree with the quote?

ANSWER KEY

UNDERSTANDING THE READING

A
1. c (Explanation: *Their job was to hunt through the garbage for…*)
2. d (Explanation: …*many catadores were proud of their work…*)
3. b (Explanation: The paragraph lists the steps that led to the creation of his artwork.)
4. e (Explanation: *Why create such huge images using garbage?*)
5. a (Explanation: The paragraph talks about the movie that followed his efforts, and how the catadores felt about the project.)

B
1. a large landfill
2. Rio de Janeiro, Brazil
3. 3,000
4. find and sell recyclable items
5. US$20–25 per day

   (Note: All of the answers can be found in Paragraphs B and C.)

C a, f, d, b, c, e

D a (Note: Although option b may seem like a valid interpretation of the quote, it is not the point the speaker intended to make.)

Writing

OVERVIEW

In this lesson, students learn more about the different elements of a paragraph. This time, the focus is on *supporting ideas* and *details*. The lesson starts by teaching students how to structure a problem/solution paragraph as preparation for the *Writing Task*. Students then learn how to structure paragraphs in general, using supporting ideas to expand on main ideas and details to expand on supporting ideas. In the *Writing Task*, students apply these lessons by writing a paragraph about an environmental problem and the various ways to improve it. Students begin the task by brainstorming for environmental problems and possible solutions, before selecting one problem and organizing the related information in an outline. Students then draft their paragraphs, improve their drafts, and correct common mistakes with introducing problems and solutions.

EXPLORING WRITTEN ENGLISH (pages 75–77)

A Noticing

In this exercise, students notice language used for describing problems and solutions. This exercise is to be done before going over the information in the *Language for Writing* box.
- Have students complete the exercise individually.
- Check answers as a class. Ask students how the language for describing problems is different from the language for describing solutions.

Language for Writing: Stating Problems and Proposing Solutions

The *Language for Writing* box explains how to start a problem/solution paragraph by introducing the problem and stating that there are solutions to the problem. It then shows students how to complete the paragraph by proposing different solutions. This structure can be used in the exercises that follow, but it will be expanded on in later sections when students learn to add details to each solution.

B Language for Writing

Students practice using the expressions from the *Language for Writing* box to complete the problem/solution paragraph. Inform students that each blank has more than one possible answer.
- Allow students time to complete the exercise individually.
- Discuss as a class. Elicit sample answers from students. Ask for different answers for each sentence. Point out how the problem is described in the first four sentences before possible solutions are mentioned in the fifth sentence.

C Language for Writing

In this exercise, students practice writing their own problem/solution sentences. First, have students complete the chart with a problem and two solutions, using brief points. Next, have them write out their ideas in complete sentences, following closely the structures used in the *Language for Writing* box.
- Allow students time to complete the task individually.
- Have them check answers in pairs.
- Discuss as a class. Elicit sample answers from students. Explain that these are now almost complete paragraphs and that all that's missing are details.

ANSWER KEY

EXPLORING WRITTEN ENGLISH

A 1. problem
  2. problem; solution
  3. problems
  4. solution
  5. solution

LANGUAGE FOR WRITING

B Answers will vary. Possible answers:
  1. problems for
  2. One solution / idea / answer is
  3. Another solution / idea / answer is (Note: *In addition, we can* is incorrect because of the infinitive form of the verb *to reuse*.)

C Answers will vary. Possible answer:
  Problem: School is far from the bus stop.
  Solution 1: Write to the bus company.
  Solution 2: Build a bridge over the railway tracks.

  Our school is quite far from the nearest bus stop, and many students arrive late for class every day. One solution is to write to the bus company and have them change the bus route. Another idea is to ask the town council to build a bridge over the railway tracks to make the walk to school shorter.

Writing Skill: Using Supporting Sentences

The *Writing Skill* box describes two types of supporting sentences: *supporting ideas* and *details*. Supporting ideas expand on main ideas. In Unit 3, students used *reasons* as supporting ideas in their paragraphs. The *Writing Skill* box explains that supporting ideas can take other forms, too. For example, in a problem/solution paragraph, each solution is a supporting idea. The box also explains that details expand on supporting ideas. This is the final ingredient students will need to form complete paragraphs. Like supporting ideas, details can take on various forms. Both details and supporting ideas can be linked using the connecting phrases taught in Units 2 and 3.

D Identifying Supporting Ideas

Students need to read the problem/solution paragraph and identify the three supporting ideas, which take the form of solutions.
- Allow students time to complete the task individually.
- Check answers as a class.

E Identifying Supporting Ideas

Students are given a topic sentence for a problem/solution paragraph. They will need to identify the three options that are suitable as supporting ideas (solutions) for the topic sentence.
- Have students complete the activity individually.
- Check answers as a class. Ask students why the other options are wrong.

F Writing Supporting Details

Students practice adding details to the three supporting ideas they identified in **E**. This is the final skill students need to write their full paragraphs.
- Allow students time to complete the task individually.
- Have them discuss their answers in pairs.
- Discuss as a class. Elicit sample answers from students, and write them on the board. Ask students to combine the topic sentence and supporting ideas from **E** with some of the details from **F** on the board and form a complete paragraph.

ANSWER KEY

WRITING SKILL

D 1. One approach is to encourage people to take public transportation.

2. Another way is to increase the cost of driving.

3. In addition, we can make residents aware of the importance…

E 2, 4, 5 (Note: Options 1 and 3 are not solutions: They do not specifically say how to get people to recycle more.)

F Answers will vary. Possible answers:

1. *(Teaching students to separate trash)* We could place recycling bins and posters in classrooms to teach children how to separate their trash.

2. *(More recycling bins to make recycling convenient)* Every bin in the city for general waste should have recycling bins next to it.

3. *(Giving people rewards for recycling)* We could have recycling collection centers throughout the city that pay people for their newspapers, soda cans, and plastic bottles.

 WRITING TASK *(page 78)*

A Brainstorming

Remind students that brainstorming is a useful first step for gathering ideas before writing. Read the *Goal* box aloud so students are familiar with the writing task before brainstorming. Students are asked to write a problem/solution paragraph about an environmental problem. Have them list two problems and as many solutions as possible for each problem.
- Allow students time to complete the task individually.
- Have students share their ideas in pairs and give each other feedback.

B Planning

Students should choose the problem with more feasible solutions. Have them create a topic sentence that states the problem and indicates that solutions are available. Next, have them complete the outline using solutions as supporting ideas and details to expand on each solution. Remind students that complete sentences are not necessary at this stage. It is more important to focus on organizing their ideas.
- Allow students time to complete their outlines individually. Provide assistance as needed.

C First Draft

Have students write first drafts of their paragraphs based on their outlines. Remind students to use the linking words and expressions they've learned to connect their ideas clearly and logically.
- Allow students time to complete the task individually. Provide assistance as needed. Refrain from error correction at this point.

ANSWER KEY

WRITING TASK

A Answers will vary. Possible answers:

Problem 1: Bad air quality caused by heavy traffic

Solutions: Better public transportation / Build offices closer to people's homes

Problem 2: People dump their trash in the rivers.

Solutions: Rubbish collection centers closer to where people live by the river / Fine people who dump their trash into the river

B Answers will vary. Possible answer:

Topic Sentence: Heavy traffic in the city results in bad air quality.

Supporting Idea: Improve public transportation so fewer people drive.

Details: Designated bus lanes, so that buses can move more quickly through traffic

REVISING PRACTICE *(page 79)*

The *Revising Practice* box contains an exercise that demonstrates several ways students can improve their first drafts.

- Allow students time to analyze the two drafts and complete the exercise.
- Check answers as a class. Ask students to identify each change and explain how it makes the revised draft stronger.

D Revised Draft

Students should apply the revision techniques used in the *Revising Practice* box to their own drafts, where applicable.

- Explain to students that they will be using the questions as a guide for checking and improving their drafts.
- As a class, go over the questions carefully to make sure students understand them.
- Allow students time to revise their paragraphs.

EDITING PRACTICE

The *Editing Practice* box trains students to spot and correct common errors related to stating problems and solutions. As a class, go over the information in the box carefully to make sure students understand what to look out for.

- Allow students time to complete the exercise individually.
- Check answers as a class by asking students to read their corrected sentences aloud and explain the errors.

ANSWER KEY

REVISING PRACTICE

   d, a, c, b

EDITING PRACTICE

1. Air pollution is a <u>problem, but</u> there are some possible solutions.
2. One solution is <u>to</u> reduce the number of cars on the roads.
3. Another solution is to <u>talk</u> to factory owners.
4. Also, we can <u>use</u> public transportation instead of driving.
5. My town has a problem with trash on the <u>streets, but</u> there are some ways to improve the situation.
6. One idea is <u>to</u> have more trash cans.
7. Another solution is to <u>tell</u> people about the problem.
8. In addition, we can <u>try</u> to recycle more.

E Final Draft

Have students apply the skills taught in *Editing Practice* to their own revised drafts and check for any other errors.

- Allow students time to edit their drafts.
- Walk around and monitor students as they work. Provide assistance as needed.
- Collect their work once they have completed it.
- For the next class, show anonymous examples of good paragraphs and common errors.

UNIT REVIEW

Students can work in groups on this recap of the unit. For question **1**, encourage students to use the target words when appropriate. For questions **2** and **3**, encourage them to check the relevant pages of the unit for answers.

- Allow students time to answer the three questions in groups.
- Ask each group to present its answer for question **1** and why they think the method will work. As a class, vote for the most effective idea.

FOOD JOURNEYS

ACADEMIC TRACK
Cultural Studies

ACADEMIC SKILLS

READING	Recognizing pronoun references
WRITING	Paraphrasing using synonyms
GRAMMAR	Giving reasons
CRITICAL THINKING	Justifying your opinion

UNIT OVERVIEW

The unit takes a look at food around the world. Students learn how cultures and environments shape the diets of people everywhere and discuss their own culinary habits.

- **READING 1:** A photographer explores the connections that link environment, food, and culture, and writes about the food in Crete.

- **VIDEO:** The same photographer visits Greenland and learns about the traditional hunting and eating habits of the Inuit.

- **READING 2:** A food blogger discusses how she and other bloggers spread cultural awareness by sharing recipes from around the world.

Students draw on what they've read and watched to write a paragraph explaining why they think people enjoy sharing pictures of food on social media. The unit prepares them by introducing useful words for talking about food and culture, and discussing the many ways food can be different and fascinating. It then teaches students how to better express their opinions by giving reasons. Finally, students learn how to write better paragraphs by using synonyms to avoid repetition.

THINK AND DISCUSS (page 81)

The photo focuses on a basket of hyacinth beans. In this photo, the beans are mostly green with striking purple edges, but sometimes, hyacinth beans can be completely purple. Hyacinth beans are also known as *lablab beans*. In India, they are used in curries, even though they are poisonous if not boiled well. The photo should get students thinking about foreign foods that they're not familiar with.

- Have students study the picture, title, and caption.
- Discuss the photo as a class. Ask students whether they have seen or eaten hyacinth beans before. Ask whether they have similar foods in their own countries.

- Discuss the questions as a class. For question **2**, ask students which dish or food pictured in the unit looks the most appealing and why.

THINK AND DISCUSS

Answers will vary. Possible answers:

1. The beans pictured are hyacinth beans. This is my first time seeing this vegetable. We have many types of green beans where I come from, but nothing as colorful as this!

2. Pages 82–83: steamed buns, pineapples, fruits and nuts, brinjal curry; Pages 85–87: Mediterranean food, snails, sardines, fava beans, traditional Greek pastries; Page 92: quinoa salad with olives and avocado; Page 95: a German cake

EXPLORE THE THEME (pages 82–83)

The photos show food from China, Cambodia, Iran, and India. *Mantou*, or steamed buns, are popular in Northern China. Brinjal (also known as eggplant) curry is popular in southern India. The photos were submitted by local photographers as part of a project to show what and how people eat in different cultures around the world.

- Allow students time to study the spread and answer the questions in pairs.
- Check answers as a class. Ask students what they think they can learn from studying food habits around the world.
- Elicit sample sentences from students for each of the blue words.

EXPLORE THE THEME

Answers will vary. Possible answers:

A 1. The photos show different foods from four different countries. The only one I have tried is pineapple.

2. I would take a photograph of my family eating out at a hawker center. Eating out is very common where I come from because the food is good and cheap, and you get to choose from many different types of dishes.

B 1. typical, share, culture

Reading 1

PREPARING TO READ (page 84)

A Building Vocabulary

The paragraph is related to the reading passage. It describes the characteristics of Mediterranean food. It also contains seven key vocabulary items that appear in the passage. Students should use contextual clues to deduce the meanings of the words.

- Have students complete the task individually.
- Check answers as a class. Elicit sample sentences for each vocabulary item.

See Vocabulary Extension 5A on page 207 of the Student Book for additional practice with words that can function as both verbs and nouns (offer, pick, taste).

B Using Vocabulary

Students should use the new vocabulary items while answering the three questions. For question **1**, explain *edible*, and provide examples, if necessary.

- Have students answer the questions in pairs.
- Discuss as a class. Elicit sample answers from students.

C Brainstorming

Students should think of as many local dishes as they can before listing six of their favorites as answers.

- Have students complete the task in pairs.
- Discuss as a class. Elicit sample answers, and ask students to describe the dishes. List them on the board, and vote to determine the most popular dish. Have students tried dishes from other countries? Which ones? How are they different?

D Predicting

The passage is about photographer Matthieu Paley, who traveled the world studying culture and cuisine, and his exploration of food and culture around the world. This is made clear by the title. The photo captions show that the passage focuses on Crete, which is in Greece. One of the captions also suggests that Cretans follow a Mediterranean diet.

- Allow students time to skim the title, photos, and captions.
- Discuss as a class. Revisit this activity after completing the passage.

ANSWER KEY

PREPARING TO READ

A **1.** prepare
  2. type
  3. fried
  4. fresh
  5. offer
  6. pick
  7. taste

B   Answers will vary. Possible answers:
  1. I grow many different types of herbs such as rosemary and thyme in my garden.
  2. I love eating fried chicken, but not too often. / I don't eat fried food at all because it's unhealthy.
  3. When people come to my home, I offer them pineapple tarts to snack on and some tea or coffee, too.

C   Answers will vary.

D   I think it's mainly about <u>Greece</u>. People probably eat <u>Mediterranean food</u> there. (Note: The Mediterranean diet is described in the paragraph in **A**. Students can list examples from there or from what they see in the photos.)

 9   Have students read the passage individually, or play the audio and have students read along.

OVERVIEW OF THE READING

The passage describes a French photographer's journey to discover more about the relationship between environment and food. Matthieu Paley visited homes in six very different countries to learn about how location affects cuisine and culture. In a journal entry about his time in Crete, Paley describes sharing a lively meal with a local family. The meal featured pies filled with the herb *horta*, snails cooked in a thick sauce, and the medicinal vegetable *avronies*.

Online search terms: traditional diet of Crete, Mediterranean diet, horta, avronies

⏱ 40 MINS **UNDERSTANDING THE READING** (page 87)

A Summarizing

Students complete a short summary of the passage by filling in the blanks with the correct options.

- Have students complete the task individually.

- Check answers as a class. Ask students where they found the answers.

B Understanding Main Ideas

The four paragraphs are all from the second part of the passage, the diary excerpt. Students are asked to identify the main idea in each paragraph.
- Have students complete the task individually.
- Check answers as a class. Ask students where they found the answers.

C Understanding Details

Students should scan the passage for the food names to find their answers.
- Have students complete the task individually.
- Check answers as a class. Ask students where they found the answers. How many of the food items listed can they spot in the photos?

D Critical Thinking: Justifying Your Opinion

The *Critical Thinking* box talks about justifying or giving reasons for an opinion. The exercise asks students to first evaluate each dish by giving it a rating and then to justify that rating by giving reasons.
- Have students complete the task individually
- Have them discuss their answers in pairs.
- Discuss as a class. Elicit sample answers from students. Vote for the most appealing dish.

DEVELOPING READING SKILLS *(page 88)*

20 MINS

Reading Skill: Recognizing Pronoun References

The *Reading Skill* box shows how to recognize the nouns that the pronouns are referring to. First, elicit examples of pronouns from students, and write them on the board. Then go over the box and the difference between subject and object pronouns. Explain that the subject of a sentence *does* the action while the object *receives* it. Recognizing a pronoun reference is easier when you can differentiate between the two types of pronouns. (Note: The pronouns *you* and *it* can operate as both subject and object pronouns.)

A Analyzing

Students are asked to spot the pronouns (both subject and object) in the paragraph and match them to the nouns they refer to. There are six pronouns in all.
- Allow students time to complete the task individually.

- Check answers as a class. Replace the pronouns with the nouns students chose, and determine whether their answers make sense.
- Ask students whether each pronoun is a subject pronoun or object pronoun and why.

B Identifying Pronoun Reference

In this exercise, the pronouns are already underlined. Students are asked to recognize the noun that each pronoun refers to.
- Allow students time to complete the exercise individually.
- Check answers as a class. Replace the pronouns with the nouns students chose, and determine whether their answers make sense.
- Ask students whether each pronoun is a subject pronoun or object pronoun and why.

Video

VIEWING: IMAGES OF GREENLAND *(pages 89–90)*

Overview of the Video

Matthieu Paley, the photographer in Reading 1, continues his food journey by learning about the food habits of the Inuit of Greenland. He stays with an Inuit family in the small, remote town of Isortoq and goes seal hunting with some of the local hunters. It takes several days before he eventually catches a seal, but in his attempts, he learns a lot about how the Inuit live and eat. In many ways, their lifestyle has remained unchanged for centuries. Paley also gets to enjoy the breathtaking scenery of the Arctic region and takes many photos of his adventure. This video was adapted from the National Geographic Live video *We Are What We Eat: Greenland*.

Online search terms: We Are What We Eat, National Geographic photographer Matthieu Paley, Inuit, Greenland

BEFORE VIEWING

A Predicting

The title states that the photo was taken in Greenland. The caption elaborates that we are looking at a specific village called Isortoq. The entire landscape is covered in snow, and the caption states that it is very cold all year-round. The fact that only 100 people live there suggests that the environment is harsh.
- Have students study the title, photo, and caption in pairs.
- Discuss as a class. Suggest different food types (fruits, vegetables, poultry, etc.), and ask students whether each one is a suitable answer.

B Learning About the Topic

The paragraph prepares students for the video by providing them with background information about the Inuit and their diet.
- Have students complete the task individually.
- Discuss as a class. Were their predictions in exercise **A** correct? Also, would students enjoy the Inuit diet? Is the changing Inuit diet good or bad for the Inuit?

C Vocabulary in Context

This exercise introduces students to some of the key words used in the video. The sentences also provide more information about the Inuit lifestyle and diet.
- Have students complete the task individually.
- Check answers as a class. Elicit sample sentences for each word.

BEFORE VIEWING

A Answers will vary. Possible answer: It looks like it's too cold for crops to grow in this village in Greenland. People there probably eat a lot of fish and meat instead.

B Answers will vary. Possible answers:

1. The Inuit diet contains much more meat than I'm used to having. / The Inuit diet doesn't contain any bread or rice, which are staples where I come from.

2. The climate, terrain, and environment shaped the traditional Inuit diet.

3. The modern Inuit diet is less limited than their traditional one. Today, the Inuit can go shopping at grocery stores for foods grown or made elsewhere.

C 1. lifestyle

2. hunt

3. remote

4. survive

WHILE VIEWING

A ▶ Understanding Main Ideas

Have students read the items before you play the video.

- Have students complete the task while the video is playing.
- Check answers as a class. Ask students why the other two options are wrong.

B ▶ Sequencing

Have students read the list of events and write any answers they recall from the first viewing before playing the video a second time.

- Have students complete the task while the video is playing.
- Check answers as a class. Draw a timeline on the board, and ask students where each event should go.

WHILE VIEWING

A a (Explanation: The narrator states this at the start of the video.)

B a, f, d, b, e, c

AFTER VIEWING

A Reacting to the Video

Students decide which of Paley's photographs in the video they remember best. Their reasons are more important than their choices. Ask students to list their reasons clearly by describing the features of the photos they remember.

- Allow students time to answer the questions individually.
- Have them discuss their answers in pairs.
- Discuss as a class. Elicit sample answers from students.

B Critical Thinking: Justifying Your Opinion

Revisit Paley's main goal in exercise **A** of the *While Viewing* section. Students should decide whether Paley achieved his goal and explain why.

- Allow students time to answer the questions individually.
- Have them discuss their answers in pairs.
- Discuss as a class. Elicit sample answers from students.

AFTER VIEWING

A Answers will vary. Possible answer: I remember the picture of the broken ice left behind by the canoe. It shows how lonely the life of an Inuit hunter is. Also, the Arctic nature in the background is very beautiful.

B Answers will vary. Possible answer: Yes. Paley saw how the constant need to search for food in the cold and challenging landscape contributes to the Inuit's hunting lifestyle. He also saw how they prepare their traditional food such as seal.

Ideas for... EXPANSION

Have students find more of Matthieu Paley's food photographs online. Some of his images can be found in the *National Geographic* article, "The Evolution of Diet." Ask students to choose one that they like and describe it to the class. Have them explain why they like it. Encourage students to include useful background information, such as when, where, and who the photo was taken with.

Reading 2

PREPARING TO READ (page 91)

A Building Vocabulary

In this exercise, the definitions of key words from the reading passage are provided. Students should use the definitions to help them complete the exercise.

• Have students complete the task individually.

• Check answers as a class. Elicit sample sentences for each vocabulary item.

See Vocabulary Extension 5B on page 207 of the Student Book for additional practice with adjectives and adverbs.

B Using Vocabulary

Students should use the new vocabulary items while answering the two questions.

• Have students work in pairs to answer the questions.

• Discuss answers as a class. Elicit answers from students. For question **1**, what was the argument about? How did it end? For question **2**, ask whether students are active on social media or blogs. Who do they follow online?

C Brainstorming

This activity gets students thinking about food blogs, the topic of Reading 2. Students should think about the type of information a food blog would contain and how the information could be useful.

• Allow students time to complete the task individually.

• Have them discuss their answers in pairs and choose their three best reasons.

• Discuss as a class. Elicit sample answers from students. Have a class vote to rank the reasons by popularity. Ask students how they feel about food blogs and people sharing photos of their meals on social media.

D Predicting

The activity's instruction line explains that the reading passage is about a food blogger. The title "Cooking the World" should therefore be enough to help students guess that she writes about food from around the world.

• Allow students time to skim the title, photos, and captions.

• Discuss as a class. Revisit this question after completing the reading.

ANSWER KEY

PREPARING TO READ

A 1. respect

2. ingredient; dish

3. recipes

4. argue

5. variety

6. hope; popular

B Answers will vary. Possible answers:

1. I once argued with someone online. I got quite angry, and neither of us changed our minds. I think most online arguments are like that.

2. I don't really pay attention to trends, but I do sometimes notice topics that are popular on Twitter. / I really like it when people create memes using scenes from popular movies.

C Answers will vary. Possible answers:

1. People want to learn new recipes.

2. People want to know the best places to eat.

3. Food blogs introduce us to dishes from around the world.

D Answers will vary. Possible answer: Martin writes about dishes and recipes from all over the world.

🎧 **10**   Have students read the passage individually, or play the audio and have students read along.

OVERVIEW OF THE READING

The reading passage consists mainly of an interview with food blogger Sasha Martin, who spent four years cooking dishes from every country in the world. By sharing the recipes she learned, she hopes to bring people of different cultures closer together by increasing their understanding and appreciation of each other. Martin believes that cooking food from different countries is a good way to learn about other places and find common ground. She chooses dishes that are easy for people of varied backgrounds to cook and enjoy in an effort to build bridges through food. The sidebar talks about the first-ever food blog and goes on to explain how the concept has evolved by showing three interesting examples.

Online search terms: Sasha Martin, Global Table Adventure, Cooking the World

UNDERSTANDING THE READING
(page 94)

A Understanding Main Ideas

Students select three main ideas that are discussed in the passage. Point out that scanning the passage for key words used in each option is a useful strategy for finding the answers.

- Allow students time to complete the task individually.
- Check answers as a class. Ask students where they found the answers.

B Understanding Details

Students match each reason to the correct blogger. The answers can be found in both the main section of the reading passage and the sidebar. Some bloggers have more than one reason.

- Allow students time to complete the task individually.
- Have them check answers in pairs.
- Discuss answers as a class. Go online and visit each blog quickly. Ask students to share their impressions.

C Understanding Pronoun Reference

Students are asked to identify the nouns that the pronouns in each sentence refer to. The three sentences are from the reading passage.

- Allow time for students to complete the task individually.
- Check answers as a class. Ask students whether the pronouns are subject or object pronouns.

D Critical Thinking: Justifying Your Opinion

The focus of this exercise should be on the reasons behind each rating.

- Allow students time to complete the exercise individually.
- Have them discuss their answers in pairs.
- Discuss as a class. Elicit sample answers from students. Find students whose rankings differ significantly, and compare their reasons. Generate a class debate based on the contrasting reasons.

Ideas for… EXPANSION

Have students describe their favorite food blogs to the class and explain why they enjoy reading them. Then have them share what they've learned from reading the blogs. Encourage listeners to ask questions. If possible, visit the blogs online as a class.

ANSWER KEY

UNDERSTANDING THE READING

A 1 (See Paragraphs B and C); 3 (See Paragraphs D and E); 4 (See Paragraph F)

B 1. c, d, g
2. f
3. e
4. b
5. a

C 1. When **Adam Roberts** was in law school, <u>he</u> (*Adam Roberts*) needed a break from studying.

2. Roberts started **a food blog** and shared <u>it</u> (*a food blog*) with other people.

3. In May of 2012, **two friends** wanted to make each other laugh, so <u>they</u> (*two friends*) created a blog for sharing pictures of ugly food.

D Answers will vary. Possible answers:

Global Table Adventure: (3) We don't get much foreign food here, and I'm curious to know what people eat around the world.

Chowhound: (2) I'm going to New York next month, so I want to know the best places to eat.

The Amateur Gourmet: (1) I don't really enjoy cooking.

Someone Ate This: (3) This blog sounds really interesting.

Kitchen Historic / Food Roots: (2) I'm interested in learning more about food people ate in the past.

Writing

OVERVIEW

In this lesson, students learn how to write a paragraph that explains something by listing reasons. The lesson starts by teaching students the language for giving reasons to support their opinions. It then goes on to explain how students can use synonyms to avoid repetitive language. In the *Writing Task*, students apply these lessons by writing a paragraph explaining why they think people enjoy posting pictures of their food online. Students begin the task by brainstorming for possible reasons before they add details to each of their reasons. Students then draft their paragraphs, improve on their drafts, and correct common mistakes with giving reasons.

EXPLORING WRITTEN ENGLISH
(pages 95–97)

A Noticing

While completing the exercise, students should notice that the words *so* and *because* can be used to show a causal relationship. *Because* introduces a reason (cause), while *so* introduces a result (effect). This exercise is to be done before going over the information in the *Language for Writing box*.

- Allow students time to complete the activity individually.
- Check answers as a class. Ask students what the sentences with the underlined words have in common.

Language for Writing: Giving Reasons

The *Language for Writing* box explains that the words *because* and *so* are used to state reasons and results. Stress that in sentences with *so*, the reason appears first and the result after it, and *so* is preceded by a comma. In sentences with *because*, it is the other way around. The box also lists other ways to introduce reasons (*one reason; another reason; to*). One expression not mentioned in the box is *so that*. If necessary, explain that this expression is not the same as *so*. *So that* introduces purpose. The purpose, or reason, appears after *so that*, not before.

B Language for Writing

Students complete the sentences by filling in the blanks with the correct words for giving reasons from the *Language for Writing box*.

- Have students complete the task individually.
- Check answers as a class. Ask students for the reason and the result in each sentence.

C Language for Writing

Each question contains two sentences: a reason and a result. Students should combine the two into a single sentence, using appropriate expressions for stating reasons. Point out that there may be more than one way to combine the sentences.

- Allow students time to complete the exercise individually.
- Discuss as a class. Ask students to identify the reason in each sentence. Elicit different ways of combining each sentence.

See Grammar Reference on pages 219–223 of the Student Book for additional information on because *and* in order to.

Writing Skill: Paraphrasing Using Synonyms

Explain to students that paragraphs are better when they contain less repetition. Students can reduce repetition and improve their paragraphs by using synonyms. Remind students that a thesaurus is a useful tool for finding synonyms and that synonyms are not always interchangeable because they often have slightly different meanings. The *Writing Skill* box contains a short paragraph that is improved by the use of synonyms.

D Writing Skill

This exercise teaches students some synonyms related to this unit's theme.

- Have students complete the task individually.
- Check answers as a class. Elicit sample sentences in which the synonyms can be used interchangeably. Ask for sample sentences in which the synonyms are <u>not</u> interchangeable.

E Writing Skill

Students paraphrase only the underlined parts of the sentences. Use question **1** as an example, if necessary. Explain that even if an underlined word has several synonyms, students should only paraphrase it in ways that sound natural.

- Allow students time to complete the exercise individually.
- Have them check answers in pairs.
- Discuss as a class. Elicit sample answers from students.

F Writing Skill

Students write a follow-up sentence that should contain at least one synonym for a word from the given sentence. Allow students to use a thesaurus, if necessary.

- Allow students time to complete the task individually. Provide assistance, if needed.
- Have them check answers in pairs.
- Discuss as a class. Elicit sample sentences from students.

ANSWER KEY

WRITING SKILL

D 1. b; **2.** f; **3.** e; **4.** i;

   5. k (Note: Although a *photo* counts as a *picture*, a *picture* doesn't always count as a *photo*. For example, a picture can also be a sketch or painting.);

   6. c (Note: *Post* here refers specifically to putting material, such as a comment or photos, online.);

   7. j; **8.** a; **9.** g; **10.** d;

   11. h (Note: A *dish* refers specifically to food items prepared and served in a meal. The word *food* includes raw ingredients, but these are not dishes.)

E Answers will vary. Possible answers:

   1. … She <u>prepared</u> <u>food</u> from 195 different countries.

   2. … she still <u>thinks</u> that <u>preparing food</u> is <u>enjoyable</u>.

   3. … Readers can <u>upload</u> their own <u>pictures</u> …

   4. … enjoy looking at the <u>images</u> of the <u>tasty dishes</u>.

F Answers will vary. Possible answers:

   1. Matthieu Paley enjoyed a <u>typical</u> Mediterranean family meal in Crete. Although it was <u>ordinary</u>, it was very delicious.

   2. Some people <u>read</u> food blogs because they want to get ideas for recipes. Others <u>visit</u> food blogs to find out about new restaurants.

WRITING TASK *(page 98)*

A Brainstorming

Remind students that brainstorming is a useful first step for gathering ideas before writing. Read the *Goal* box aloud so students are familiar with the writing task before brainstorming. Students should list at least three reasons why people post photos of their food online, either on social media or on blogs. Several are already given, and others can be found in Reading 2. Ideas should be briefly worded. They need not be listed in any order.

- Allow students time to complete the task individually.
- Have students discuss their ideas in pairs and give each other feedback.

B Planning

Students should first decide whether they want to focus on social media or on blogs. They should then come up with an appropriate topic sentence. Next, have them choose their three best reasons from exercise **A** and add details to each. Remind students that complete sentences are not necessary at this stage. It is more important to focus on organizing their ideas.

- Allow students time to complete their outlines individually. Provide assistance as needed.

C First Draft

Have students write first drafts of their paragraphs based on their outlines.

- Allow students time to complete the task individually. Provide assistance as needed. Refrain from error correction at this point.

WRITING TASK

A Answers will vary. Possible answers:

show off their cooking skills / keep a record of something interesting they've eaten / make others jealous / recommend a new restaurant

B Answers will vary. Possible answer:

Topic Sentence: There are many reasons why people share food photos on their blogs.

Supporting Idea 1: Show off their cooking skills

Detail: It's natural to feel proud after cooking a new dish for the first time.

Supporting Idea 2: Keep a record of an interesting meal

Details: I once posted a photo of stir-fried jellyfish I was served at a Vietnamese restaurant.

Suppporting Idea 3: Share information about a great restaurant

Details: I once wrote about an Italian restaurant I liked and also posted photos of the food to recommend the place to my friends.

REVISING PRACTICE   *(page 99)*

The *Revising Practice* box contains an exercise that demonstrates several ways students can improve their first drafts.

- Allow students time to analyze the two drafts and complete the exercise.
- Check answers as a class. Ask students to identify each change and explain how it makes the revised draft stronger.

D Revised Draft

Students should apply the revision techniques used in the *Revising Practice* box to their own drafts, where applicable.

- Explain to students that they will be using the questions as a guide for checking and improving their drafts.
- As a class, go over the questions carefully to make sure students understand them.
- Allow students time to revise their paragraphs.

EDITING PRACTICE

The *Editing Practice* box trains students to spot and correct common errors with giving reasons. As a class, go over the information in the box carefully to make sure students understand what to look out for.

- Allow students time to complete the exercise individually.
- Check answers as a class by asking students to read their corrected sentences aloud and explain the errors.

REVISING PRACTICE

d, c, b, a

EDITING PRACTICE

1. Some people want to share their good eating <u>habits, so</u> they post pictures of their meals on social media.

2. I think people post pictures of the food they make to <u>share</u> their hobby with their friends.

3. Food blogger Clotilde Dusoulier quit her job <u>because</u> she wanted to become a full-time food writer.

4. Because they want to make some <u>money, some</u> food bloggers have ads on their sites.

5. People read food <u>blogs because</u> they need ideas for things to make for dinner.

6. Some people post pictures of their food to <u>tell</u> people about new restaurants in town.

E Final Draft

Have students apply the skills taught in *Editing Practice* to their own revised drafts and check for any other errors.

- Allow students time to edit their drafts.
- Walk around and monitor students as they work. Provide assistance as needed.
- Collect their work once they have completed it.
- For the next class, show anonymous examples of good paragraphs and common errors.

UNIT REVIEW

Students can work in groups on this recap of the unit. For question **1**, encourage students to use the target words when appropriate. For questions **2** and **3**, encourage them to check the relevant pages of the unit for answers.

- Allow students time to answer the three questions in groups.
- Ask each group to share its answer for question **1**.

Ideas for... **EXPANSION**

Have students create a food blog as a class. Ask students to work in pairs or small groups. Have each group write a blog entry about a dish that they feel represents their culture. Students should include some background information about the dish, a recipe, as well as pictures of the food. Upload the stories and pictures to the blog site, and share the blog with the rest of the school.

FUTURE LIVING

ACADEMIC TRACK

Engineering / Technology

ACADEMIC SKILLS

READING	Identifying examples
WRITING	Using pronouns to avoid repetition
GRAMMAR	Using *and, but,* and *so*
CRITICAL THINKING	Inferring attitude

UNIT OVERVIEW

This unit explores how advancing technology will change our lives in the future. From sociable robots that take care of us to smart homes to making Mars habitable, technology is moving us into a future with many new and exciting opportunities.

- **READING 1:** In the future, smart homes will have appliances that communicate with each other and robot caregivers that tend to our needs.

- **VIDEO:** Advocates of colonizing Mars discuss why manned missions to the red planet are possible, beneficial, and necessary.

- **READING 2:** In order to colonize Mars, steps must be taken to warm the planet, fill it with oxygen, and make it more suitable for humans.

Students draw on what they've read and watched to write a paragraph about what daily life in 2050 will be like. The unit prepares them by introducing vocabulary to talk about technology and discussing advances in technology. Students learn how to connect related information using conjunctions and how to use pronouns to avoid repetition. Students also learn phrases that are used to introduce examples.

THINK AND DISCUSS (page 101)

The photo shows a couple getting married in Tokyo, Japan. The wedding was the first ever to be officiated by a robot. The photo is meant to get students thinking about the different ways technology will affect our lives in the future.

- Have students study the picture, title, and caption.
- Discuss the photo as a class. What are students' thoughts about robot-officiated weddings?
- Discuss the questions as a class. Before discussing question **1**, ask students how technology has affected our lives in the last 50 years. For question **2**, ask students what influenced their opinion (for example, movies, history, or an interview).

ANSWER KEY

THINK AND DISCUSS

Answers will vary. Possible answers:

1. I think all cars will be driverless in 50 years. In 100 years, driverless cars will probably be able to fly.

2. Living on other planets will probably be too difficult. We will be able to visit these planets, but I don't think we'll ever stay there. / I'm sure that we'll discover a planet similar to Earth one day and that we'll find a way to get there and live there, too.

EXPLORE THE THEME (pages 102–103)

The opening spread features an infographic predicting how technology will change city life. The ideas mentioned include driverless cars, underground bike lanes, wearable technology, and personalized advertising.

- Allow students time to study the spread and answer the questions individually.
- Check answers as a class. Ask students whether they dislike any of the ideas mentioned. For example, discuss the advantages and disadvantages of the type of personalized advertising shown in the spread.
- Elicit sample sentences from students for each of the blue words.

ANSWER KEY

EXPLORE THE THEME

A Answers will vary. Possible answers:

1. I think driverless cars will improve our lives the most. There will be fewer traffic jams and road accidents once all the cars on the road are able to communicate with each other. Traveling will also be much less stressful!

2. Many companies are already selling wearable technology such as smart watches. / Driverless cars and buses are also being tested in many places. / Solar panels are being used much more frequently in cities and small towns. / Underground trains and pedestrian paths can already be found in many cities.

B adapt; technology; predict

Reading 1

30 MINS PREPARING TO READ *(page 104)*

A Building Vocabulary

The sentences are about technological advancements happening now. They contain seven key vocabulary items that appear in the passage. Students should use contextual clues to deduce the meanings of the words.
- Have students complete the exercise individually.
- Check answers as a class. Elicit sample sentences for each vocabulary item.

See Vocabulary Extension 6A on page 208 of the Student Book for additional practice with the suffix -able (sociable, suitable).

B Using Vocabulary

Students should use the new vocabulary item while answering the two questions.

Explain that intelligent devices are the same as smart devices.
- Have students answer the questions in pairs.
- Discuss as a class. Ask students what makes a device *smart* or *intelligent*.

C Brainstorming

Students should think of technological advancements and place them in the correct categories. If necessary, limit students to developments made in the last 20 years.
- Allow students time to create their lists in pairs.
- Discuss as a class. Elicit sample answers from students. List them on the board, and vote as a class to decide which development is the most useful and which is the most entertaining.

D Predicting

The passage is about how technology will change homes in the future. While students are skimming the passage, the headings will provide them with the biggest clues, as they break the passage into three sections.
- Allow students time to complete the task individually.
- Have students discuss their answers in pairs.
- Discuss as a class. Revisit this activity after completing the reading.

ANSWER KEY

PREPARING TO READ

A 1. link

   2. sociable (Note: *Sociable* is normally used to describe people or animals, not robots.)

   3. preference

   4. suggest

   5. intelligent

   6. network

   7. store

B   Answers will vary. Possible answers:

   I use my smartphone every day to surf the Internet and watch videos online. I also use it to share photos and messages with my friends. / I recently bought an intelligent vacuum cleaner. I can control it from anywhere through the Internet. It's programmed to clean my house every day at 3 p.m., and it sends me an update as soon as it's done.

C   Answers will vary. Possible answers:

   Easier: computers, cell phones, robotic machinery, electric bicycles

   More fun: virtual reality video games, remote control drone aircraft, smart TVs

D   2, 3, 4

🎧 **11**   Have students read the passage individually, or play the audio and have students read along.

OVERVIEW OF THE READING

The passage describes some features that homes in the future are likely to have. These features make use of technologies that already exist today. People will interact more with their homes and appliances, which will use RFID chips and OLED displays to allow for a high degree of customization. In addition, sociable robots will do housework, take care of family members, and interact with people in human-like ways.

Online search terms: smart homes, RFID chip, OLED, social robots

40 MINS UNDERSTANDING THE READING
(page 107)

A Understanding Main Ideas

Students are asked to match paragraphs in the passage to their main ideas.
- Allow students time to complete the task individually.
- Check answers as a class. Ask students where they found the answers.

B Understanding Details

Students are asked to determine whether various statements are true or false, according to the passage.

Explain that they should mark a statement as "NG" if there isn't enough information in the passage that supports it.
- Allow students time to complete the task individually.
- Have them check answers in pairs.
- Discuss as a class. Ask students where they found the answers. Ask them how to make each false statement true.

C Critical Thinking: Inferring Attitude

The *Critical Thinking* box describes how to infer an author's attitude, or guess how the author feels about a topic. The author's attitude may not be directly stated, but it can often be inferred from word choice. For example, if most of the modifiers are positive, the author's attitude is likely positive, too. For the exercise, have students guess *positive* or *negative* based on their initial reading of the passage. Then have them look for supporting sentences from the passage. Finally, ask students to revise their answers, if necessary.
- Allow students time to complete the task in pairs.
- Check answers as a class. Elicit sentences that communicate the author's attitude.

D Critical Thinking: Applying

For question **1**, students are likely to want most or all of the technologies described in the passage in their own homes. Try limiting students to one or two choices, or ask them to rank the technologies in order of preference. For question **2**, encourage students to think of technologies that haven't been invented yet.
- Allow students time to complete the task in pairs.
- Discuss as a class. Elicit sample answers from students. Have students explain their answers. For question **1**, is there any technology they would not like in their homes? For question **2**, vote as a class for the best "invention."

ANSWER KEY

UNDERSTANDING THE READING

A **1.** E (Explanation: *This intelligent technology works like a computer "brain" that controls your entire house.*)

2. C (Explanation: While Paragraph B explains that appliances will communicate with us, Paragraph C explains that RFID technology makes this possible.)

3. D (Explanation: OLED screens will function as windows or walls and allow us to change the appearance and colors of houses instantly.)

4. H (Explanation: *There's a good chance it will be a part of your life in the next 10 years…*)

5. G (Explanation: Sociable robots with the ability to express feelings will do housework and take care of children and the elderly.)

B **1.** T (See Paragraphs B and C)

2. F (See Paragraph C)

3. NG (Explanation: This topic is not covered in the reading passage.)

4. T (See Paragraph E)

5. T (See Paragraph G)

6. T (See Paragraphs F and G)

C Answers will vary. Possible answer:

Positive: In Paragraph A, the author uses very positive phrases such as *soft light*, *favorite breakfast*, and *perfect temperature*. In addition, the writer only stresses the advantages of new technology and does not mention possible disadvantages.

D Answers will vary. Possible answers:

1. I would like to have OLED walls. I once painted my room, and it took me a few days to finish. I would like to change my wall color more frequently, but painting is too much work. OLED walls would solve my problem.

2. Technology that notices when you're running low on supplies, such as toilet paper or toothpaste, and orders them for you online. / A robot that walks and feeds the dog. / Electric outlets that turn off automatically once devices have been charged.

⏱ 20 MINS DEVELOPING READING SKILLS *(page 108)*

Reading Skill: Identifying Examples

The *Reading Skill* box shows several ways to introduce an example. *For instance* and *for example* can be used interchangeably, typically at the start of a sentence, followed by a comma. *Such as* appears in the middle of a sentence. It connects a statement to supporting examples within the same sentence. A comma usually comes before it.

A Identifying Examples

The paragraph describes what the sociable robot Wakamaru is able to do by giving examples. Students are asked to spot the phrases that introduce these examples and identify the examples themselves.
- Have students complete the task individually.
- Check answers as a class.

B Identifying Examples

Students elaborate on sentences by matching them to corresponding examples. The examples and the sentences should describe related things. Also, the way the two parts connect should be grammatically correct.

- Have students complete the task individually.
- Check answers as a class. Ask students to explain how the use of *for instance* in option b is different from its use in previous sentences. Have students come up with their own ideas using *for instance* and *for example* in the middle of a sentence.

C Introducing Examples

Students now get to practice creating and introducing their own examples using the expressions taught. Ask students to pay attention to how the stem in each item ends (with a period or a comma).

- Allow students time to complete the exercise individually.
- Discuss as a class. Elicit sample answers from students. Ask for different ways to introduce students' examples by changing the phrasing.

ANSWER KEY

DEVELOPING READING SKILLS

A **For instance**, <u>Wakamaru can recognize faces, use gestures, and understand 10,000 Japanese words</u>.

   ...such as <u>the weather and the news</u>.

   For example, <u>at night, it moves quietly around the house, but it can wake family members up if there is any trouble</u>.

B **1.** e;   **2.** a;   **3.** d;   **4.** b;   **5.** c

C Answers will vary. Possible answers:

   1. I think living in a smart home would make life more convenient. <u>For instance, I wouldn't have to go to the supermarket to buy groceries anymore. The house would automatically order what I need online and have the items delivered.</u>

   2. I would like to live with a robot. I would ask it to do many things, <u>such as chores and shopping</u>.

Ideas for... EXPANSION

Have students work in pairs or small groups to go online and research other sociable robots like Wakamaru. Have them prepare short presentations to introduce the robots and explain their functions. Students should include examples and list them using the phrases taught in the previous exercises.

Video

VIEWING: LIVING ON MARS
(pages 109–110)

Overview of the Video

Although there have been several unmanned missions to Mars, there have been no attempts to send people there yet. Sending people to Mars is thought to be too expensive and dangerous, but Dr. Bob Zubrin strongly believes that there are ways to put people on Mars in an affordable and safe way. Even if we do manage to do this, living on Mars will be difficult because of its cold temperature and lack of oxygen and liquid water. Dr. Chris McKay believes that we can solve these problems by warming up Mars's atmosphere with greenhouse gases and by using cyanobacteria to create oxygen.

Online search terms: Mars Society, colonizing Mars, SpaceX

BEFORE VIEWING

A Predicting

From the photo, students should be able to infer that it is very dry on Mars. Students may have even read or watched videos debating whether water exists in liquid form on Mars. Encourage students to draw on their own knowledge to predict some of the other challenges of living on Mars, like its lack of oxygen, its cold temperature, and its distance from Earth. These are not evident from just the photo and title.

- Have students study the title, photo, and caption in pairs.
- Discuss as a class. Will humans ever be able to overcome these challenges, and do we really need to?

B Learning About the Topic

The paragraph provides students with reasons why Mars is suitable for humans to live on. Ask students to identify the three main reasons and summarize them in their own words.

- Allow students time to complete the task individually.
- Have them check answers in pairs.
- Discuss as a class. Ask students to share any other information they have about Mars.

C Vocabulary in Context

This exercise introduces students to some of the key words used in the video. The paragraph also provides more information about missions to Mars.

- Allow students time to complete the task individually.
- Check answers as a class. Elicit sample sentences for each word.

BEFORE VIEWING

A   Answers will vary. Possible answers: lack of oxygen, food, and water / the distance between Earth and Mars / the difference in gravity on Mars / the cold temperature

B   Answers will vary. Possible answers:

1. The length of a day on Mars is also about 24 hours.

2. Mars gets enough light from the sun for people to use solar panels.

3. In our solar system, Mars's temperature is closest to Earth's.

C 1. atmosphere

2. colonize (Note: In the paragraph, *colonize* means to start a sustainable living community on Mars. Teachers may also wish to explain the other sense of the word: when one country claims political control over another.)

3. mission

4. ambitious (Note: An *ambitious plan* is a difficult one. An *ambitious person* is someone who is determined to succeed.)

WHILE VIEWING

A ▶ Understanding Main Ideas

Have students read the items before you play the video.
- Have them complete the task while the video is playing.
- Check answers as a class. Have students explain the answers.

B ▶ Understanding Details

Have students read the question and write any answers they recall from the first viewing before playing the video a second time.
- Have students complete the task while the video plays.
- Check answers in pairs before discussing answers as a class.

WHILE VIEWING

A 1. Dr. Zubrin (Explanation: *We should have been on Mars a quarter century ago.*)

2. Dr. Zubrin (Explanation: *Zubrin is also doing research to prepare for a manned mission to Mars.*)

3. Dr. McKay (Explanation: *He wants to create an atmosphere on Mars so humans can live there.*)

B   2, 4, 5 (Explanation: McKay claims that we can warm Mars by introducing greenhouse gases and can create oxygen by using cyanobacteria.)

AFTER VIEWING

A Reacting to the Video

Students are asked to evaluate the ambitions of Dr. Zubrin and Dr. McKay. Is visiting and colonizing Mars a good idea?
- Have students complete the task in pairs.
- Discuss as a class. Elicit sample answers from students. Have students with opposing viewpoints discuss and debate their reasons.

B Critical Thinking: Synthesizing

Have students skim through Reading 1. Then ask them to imagine living on Mars. What would they want or need while there? Which technologies from the reading would help them fulfill those wants and needs?
- Allow students time to complete the exercise individually.
- Have them discuss their answers in pairs. Each pair should select its two best ideas.
- Discuss as a class. Elicit sample answers from students. Vote as a class on the most useful technology.

AFTER VIEWING

A   Answers will vary. Possible answers: Yes, I do. There are probably resources on Mars that will benefit humans. Also, we need a second home in case anything happens to Earth. / Definitely not. I think it's too expensive, and we should focus on solving our problems here on Earth. Besides, traveling to Mars could be dangerous.

B   Answers will vary. Possible answers: OLED walls could create virtual windows that show us scenes from Earth so that we don't feel so homesick. / Having to wear a spacesuit every time we need to go outside would be quite inconvenient. Sociable robots that can handle simple outdoor tasks would therefore be very useful.

Reading 2

PREPARING TO READ *(page 111)*

30 MINS

A Building Vocabulary

The paragraph is about changing Mars to make it habitable. It contains five key vocabulary items that appear in the passage. Students should use contextual clues to deduce the meanings of the words.

- Have students complete the exercise individually.
- Check answers as a class. Elicit sample sentences for each vocabulary item.

See Vocabulary Extension 6B on page 208 of the Student Book for additional practice with the suffix -ment (equipment, measurement).

B Building Vocabulary

Students should first use a dictionary to check the definitions of the three words in blue before using the words to complete the sentences.

- Have them complete the task individually.
- Check answers as a class. Elicit sample sentences for each vocabulary item.

C Using Vocabulary

Students should use the new vocabulary items while answering the two questions. For question **2**, explain that there are different types of environments on Earth and that different plants grow in them. Give one or two examples, if necessary.

- Have students answer the questions in pairs.
- Discuss as a class. Elicit sample answers from students.

D Predicting

The title should serve as a very big clue for students. In addition, the numbers in the photo suggest that a process is being represented. The image on the spread illustrates this process. As we move from left to right, the image shows Mars becoming a more habitable place. Students should conclude from having watched the video and read the the paragraph in exercise **A** that the passage is about making Mars habitable.

- Allow time for students to study the title and image.
- Discuss as a class. Revisit the question after completing the reading.

 12 Have students read the passage individually, or play the audio and have students read along.

OVERVIEW OF THE READING

The passage describes how Mars can be transformed into a planet that humans can successfully and safely inhabit. The process will probably take more than 1,000 years. It would first involve introduction of greenhouse gases to raise the temperature on Mars to match Earth's. Mars's ice would eventually turn to water, which would allow plants to grow and produce oxygen. However, people would probably still need special breathing equipment to survive on the planet. The reading and graphics were adapted from the National Geographic article "The Big Idea—Making Mars the New Earth" by Robert Kunzig.

Online search terms: Making Mars the New Earth, National Geographic Mars

UNDERSTANDING THE READING *(page 114)*

40 MINS

A Understanding Main Ideas

Students are asked to identify three main ideas from the passage to complete a summary.

- Have students complete the task individually.
- Check answers as a class. Ask students where they found the answers.

B Sequencing

Students complete a timeline for colonizing Mars using details from the passage. The information comes mainly from Paragraphs D to H, but students must infer the correct order themselves. Go over the meaning of the word *terraform*, if necessary.

- Allow students time to complete the task individually.
- Check answers as a class. Have students explain their reasoning. For example, it would not be possible to build factories unless you first have homes for the people who build them.

C Identifying Problems and Solutions

Students are asked to spot a solution and a problem from the passage. Note that for question **1**, solar power was presented as a feasible power source in exercise **B** of *Before Viewing*. This is not mentioned in Reading 2, but is an acceptable answer.

- Have students complete the task individually.
- Check answers as a class. Ask where students found the answers. Is there a solution for question **2**'s answer?

D Critical Thinking: Justifying Your Opinion

Have students search online for companies that are selling people tickets to Mars. Have them find out some of the details about these future missions. Ask students whether any of the missions sound appealing.

- Allow students time to complete the task in pairs or small groups.
- Discuss as a class. Elicit sample answers from students. Have students with opposing viewpoints discuss and debate their reasons. Conduct a poll to see how many would be in favor of going to Mars.

UNDERSTANDING THE READING

A 2, 4, 5 (Note: Although 1 and 3 are mentioned in the passage, neither is a main idea that should be included in a summary.)

B c, a, e, f, b, d

C **1.** Nuclear power and wind turbines are two possible sources of power on Mars.

2. Even after 1,000 years, there will still not be enough oxygen on Mars for humans to breathe. (Note: The solution to this is mentioned in Paragraph J.)

D Answers will vary. Possible answer: I'm not sure. Life on Mars sounds hard. I don't think I'd be interested in living there for a long time. However, I'd like to travel there and stay there for a short time. That would be a fun adventure, I think.

Ideas for… EXPANSION

Visit the Mars Society website as a class, and discuss any new developments for the first manned mission to Mars. Has it made any progress? Are things happening faster than expected? Does a manned mission to Mars seem more or less likely?

Writing

OVERVIEW

In this lesson, students learn how to write better paragraphs by connecting information and avoiding repetition. The lesson starts by explaining how to use conjunctions to link ideas. Students then learn how to use pronouns to avoid repetition. In the *Writing Task*, students apply these lessons by writing a paragraph describing what a typical day in 2050 will be like. Students begin the task by brainstorming for ideas, organizing their ideas into categories, and adding details to each idea. Students then draft their paragraphs, improve their drafts, and correct common mistakes related to the use of conjunctions and pronouns.

EXPLORING WRITTEN ENGLISH
(pages 115–117)

A Noticing

Students should notice how the conjunctions *and*, *but*, and *so* join ideas in different ways. This exercise is to be done before going over the information in the *Language for Writing* box.

- Have students complete the task individually.
- Check answers as a class. For each correct option, ask students to point out the word that shows the relationship between the underlined idea and the rest of the sentence. Ask students whether they know the name for words like these.

Language for Writing: Using *And*, *But*, and *So*

The *Language for Writing* box explains how *and*, *but*, and *so* connect ideas differently. *And* shows that a linked idea is additional. *But* shows that it is a contrasting idea. *So* shows that it is a result. Explain that commas should be used before conjunctions when they link entire clauses, or parts of a sentence that contain both a subject and a predicate. Also, explain that when the subject or an auxiliary verb (such as *will* or *may*) is repeated in the same sentence, it can be dropped in the second clause once the sentences are combined.

B Language for Writing

Students complete the sentences by filling in the blanks with the correct conjunctions.

- Allow students time to complete the task individually.
- Check answers as a class. Ask students to state whether the linked idea is *additional*, *contrasting*, or a *result* before giving their answers.

C Language for Writing

Students practice joining sentences using the three conjunctions. Some questions contain a repeated auxiliary verb or subject. Point out that for this exercise, these should be dropped. Go over the example. Both *They* (subject) and *can* (auxiliary verb) from the second sentence are dropped when the sentences are combined.

- Allow students time to complete the task individually.
- Check answers as a class. Elicit sample sentences from students. Ask for possible variations. Ask other students whether these variations are incorrect or acceptable.

D Language for Writing

Students work in pairs to complete the chart before they write a sentence about their ideas using the conjunctions *and*, *but*, and *so*.

- Allow students time to complete the task in pairs.
- Discuss as a class. Have each pair present its best answer.

See Grammar Reference on pages 219–223 of the Student Book for additional information on the coordinating conjunctions and, but, *and* so.

ANSWER KEY

EXPLORING WRITTEN ENGLISH

A 1. a
2. b
3. b

B 1. so
2. and
3. and
4. but
5. so
6. but
7. but
8. so

C 1. PR2—a robot—can take care of elderly people <u>and</u> deliver mail.
2. PR2 cooks <u>but</u> doesn't communicate.
3. Wakamaru knows 10,000 Japanese words <u>and</u> is able to communicate with people.
4. There is not enough oxygen on Mars, <u>so</u> humans cannot breathe there.

D Answers will vary. Possible answers: Cars in the future will be able to fly, but they will also be driverless, so we won't need pilot licenses to use them! (Note: Use this to show students that more than two ideas can be combined by using more than one conjunction.)

Writing Skill: Using Pronouns to Avoid Repetition

Remind students that they learned to use synonyms to avoid repetition in Unit 5. The *Writing Skill* box teaches them to use pronouns for the same purpose. Refresh their memories by asking for examples of pronouns. Remind students that pronouns can be used in place of both subjects and objects. Point out that pronouns, like synonyms, can help make writing sound better and more interesting. Students should, however, avoid unclear pronoun references.

E Writing Skill

Students reduce repetition in the sentences by canceling out repeated words and replacing them with suitable pronouns.
- Allow students time to complete the task individually.
- Check answers as a class.

F Writing Skill

Students practice identifying pronoun references. Remind students that this was taught in Unit 5.
- Allow students time to complete the task individually.
- Check answers as a class.

ANSWER KEY

WRITING SKILL

E 1. RFID chips will keep track of the food in your cabinets, and <u>they</u> will tell you when it's time to go to the store.

 2. People on survey missions to Mars will build domes and live in <u>them</u>.

 3. People will terraform Mars and make <u>it</u> more like Earth.

 4. Even after a thousand years, people won't be able to breathe on Mars, so <u>they</u> will have to use breathing equipment.

 5. Mars doesn't have any oxygen, but plants will slowly add <u>it</u> to the atmosphere over many years.

F 1. they = the robots; them = people

 2. them = the domes

 3. it = the color

 4. they = people

WRITING TASK *(page 118)*

A Brainstorming

Remind students that brainstorming is a useful first step for gathering ideas before writing. Read the *Goal* box aloud so students are familiar with the writing task before brainstorming. Have students think of two ideas for each category and try to come up with one or two of their own categories, too. Ideas should be briefly worded. They need not be listed in any order.
- Allow students time to complete the task individually.
- Have students discuss their ideas in pairs and give each other feedback.

B Planning

Students choose the three categories that contain their best ideas and use each category as a supporting idea. The ideas they listed for each category form the details. Point out that students can use the expressions for introducing examples covered in *Reading Skill* to introduce their ideas if they wish to do so. Remind students that complete sentences are not necessary. Students should focus more on organizing their ideas.
- Allow students time to complete the task individually. Provide assistance as needed.

C First Draft

Have students write first drafts of their paragraphs based on their outlines. Remind students to connect related ideas using appropriate conjunctions and to avoid unnecessary repetition.
- Allow students time to complete the task individually. Provide assistance as needed. Refrain from error correction at this point.

WRITING TASK

A Answers will vary. Possible answers:

Work: Most people will work from home.

Travel: electric cars, high-speed trains

Home: automated robotic appliances to clean the house

B Answers will vary. Possible answer:

Supporting Idea 1: Travel will be cleaner and faster.

Detail: Electric cars will be cleaner and much quieter; driverless cars will communicate with each other and reduce traffic congestion.

Supporting Idea 2: Life at home after work will be much easier.

Detail: Robotic cleaners that vacuum and mop will save us a lot of time; We will be able to program our appliances to prepare us meals every day.

REVISING PRACTICE *(page 119)*

The *Revising Practice* box contains an exercise that demonstrates several ways students can improve their first drafts.

- Allow students time to analyze the two drafts and complete the exercise.
- Check answers as a class. Ask students to identify each change and explain how it makes the revised draft stronger.

D Revised Draft

Students should apply the revision techniques used in the *Revising Practice* box to their own drafts, where applicable.

- Explain to students that they will be using the questions as a guide for checking and improving their drafts.
- As a class, go over the questions carefully to make sure students understand them.
- Allow students time to revise their paragraphs.

EDITING PRACTICE

The *Editing Practice* box trains students to spot and correct common errors related to the use of *and*, *but*, and *so*. As a class, go over the information in the box carefully to make sure students understand what to look out for.

- Allow students time to complete the exercise individually.
- Check answers as a class by asking students to read their corrected sentences aloud and explain the errors.

REVISING PRACTICE

c, b, a, d

EDITING PRACTICE

1. People will live on Mars someday, <u>but</u> it is too expensive to travel there now.
2. Mars is too cold for human visitors, <u>so</u> scientists will need to warm it up.
3. Robots will take care of children <u>and</u> do housework.
4. A trip to Mars sounds amazing, <u>but</u> I would not like to live there!
5. Smart appliances will buy food <u>and</u> cook dinner.
6. We might have flying cars in 2050, <u>so</u> there might be fewer cars on our roads.
7. In the future, you might have a language chip in your brain, <u>so</u> you won't have to study foreign languages.

E Final Draft

Have students apply the skills taught in *Editing Practice* to their own revised drafts and check for any other errors.

- Allow students time to edit their drafts.
- Walk around and monitor students as they work. Provide assistance as needed.
- Collect their work once they have completed it.
- For the next class, show anonymous examples of good paragraphs and common errors.

UNIT REVIEW

Students can work in groups on this recap of the unit. For question **1**, encourage students to use the target words when appropriate. For questions **2** and **3**, encourage them to check the relevant pages of the unit for answers.

- Allow students time to answer the three questions in groups. For question **1**, ask students to include their own ideas on how the future will likely be different.
- Ask each group to present its answer for **1**. As a class, vote for the most interesting prediction for the future.

EXPLORATION

ACADEMIC TRACK
Earth Science

ACADEMIC SKILLS

READING	Identifying facts and speculations
WRITING	Introducing examples
GRAMMAR	Expressing interests and desires
CRITICAL THINKING	Understanding analogies

UNIT OVERVIEW

The theme of this unit is exploration on our planet, both underground and under the sea. Exploration requires courage, as well as curiosity, but the rewards are often spectacular. Students learn how exploration can lead to important and stunning discoveries that change what we know about the world.

- **READING 1:** A homeowner and construction workers discover two ancient underground cities in Turkey.

- **VIDEO:** A group of cavers explore one of the world's largest caves in Vietnam.

- **READING 2:** Scientists explore blue holes—spectacular underwater caves with harsh but unique environments.

Students draw on what they've read and watched to write a paragraph about a place they would like to explore. The unit prepares them for the writing task by introducing vocabulary to talk about exploration, teaching expressions for talking about interests and desires, and showing how to introduce examples in their writing. Students also learn how to distinguish between statements of fact and speculation.

 THINK AND DISCUSS (page 121)

The picture is of a diver investigating a cow's skull in an underwater cave in Mexico. The photo suggests that *explorers* include scientists and researchers who study unfamiliar parts of already well-known places. This is an idea covered in the unit. Director James Cameron is an example mentioned in *Explore the Theme*.

- Have students study the picture, title, and caption.
- Discuss the photo as a class. How did the cow skull find its way under the sea?
- Discuss the questions as a class. For question **1**, ask whether the diver is considered an explorer. For question **2**,

point out that exploring a place (for example, a shopping mall) doesn't necessarily make you an explorer.

ANSWER KEY

THINK AND DISCUSS

Answers will vary. Possible answers:

1. The Italian explorer Marco Polo is famous for his journey through Asia. / Chinese explorer Zheng He led many ships across the sea to Africa.

2. I would love to explore our mysterious oceans! / I went to Bali once, but there are so many other islands in Indonesia worth exploring.

 EXPLORE THE THEME (pages 122–123)

The opening spread is about the Mariana Trench. It is the deepest place in the world, stretching 11 kilometers down into the Pacific Ocean. The infographic helps students visualize this by comparing it to Mount Everest. It also illustrates how far down humans have gone in submarines. James Cameron's expedition to the bottom was recorded for the documentary *Deep Sea Challenge*.

- Allow students time to study the spread.
- Discuss the photo as a class. Why is it difficult to get to the bottom of the trench? What do students think they'd find there?
- Discuss the questions as a class. Elicit sample sentences from students for each of the blue words.

ANSWER KEY

EXPLORE THE THEME

A Answers will vary. Possible answers:

1. The Mariana Trench is an underwater valley that is 11 kilometers deep. It is special because the bottom of the trench is the deepest place on Earth.

2. Film director James Cameron made it to the bottom of the trench alone in 2012.

B located; experience; deep

Ideas for… EXPANSION

Have students watch short clips or trailers of James Cameron's documentary *Deep Sea Challenge* online. Discuss whether they would like to explore the trench themselves in a submarine.

Reading 1

PREPARING TO READ *(page 124)*

30 MINS

A Building Vocabulary

The paragraph is loosely related to the reading passage. It describes how archaeologists discovered a lost city in Honduras. It also contains seven key vocabulary items that appear in the passage. Students should use contextual clues to deduce the meanings of the words.

- Have students complete the task individually.
- Check answers as a class. Elicit sample sentences for each vocabulary item.

See Vocabulary Extension 7A on page 209 of the Student Book for additional practice with adjectives and nouns that describe measurements (high, height, long, length).

B Using Vocabulary

Students should use the new vocabulary items while answering the questions.

- Have students answer the questions in pairs. For question **2**, ask students to also discuss why they want to visit each region.
- Discuss as a class. Elicit sample answers from students.

C Predicting

The photo is of Turkey's "fairy chimneys" in Cappadocia. The region is also famous for Derinkuyu, one of the underground cities described in the passage.

- Allow time for students to look at the title, photo, and captions.
- Have students discuss their answers in pairs.
- Discuss as a class. Revisit this activity after completing the reading.

ANSWER KEY

PREPARING TO READ

A 1. region (Note: The term *region* is often modified by a location or direction or some other word stating a feature of the region. Examples: Arctic region, eastern region, desert region)

    2. discover (Note: When you discover something, you are either the first to find it or you are personally finding out about something for the first time.)

    3. ancient

    4. massive

    5. hidden

    6. underground

    7. artifact

B   Answers will vary. Possible answers:

    1. There is a tunnel in town that stretches from the train station to several different malls. Since it is underground, the temperature is usually cool inside.

    2. I live in the northern region of my country. I'd like to explore some of my country's islands down in the southern region.

C   Answers will vary. Possible answer:

    I think the cities were built in caves and used for hiding from other groups of people.

🎧 13 Have students read the passage individually, or play the audio and have students read along.

OVERVIEW OF THE READING

The passage talks about how the giant underground city Derinkuyu was discovered in 1963 in Cappadocia, Turkey, by an ordinary man renovating his home. The city is believed to have been a refuge for residents during attacks. It was thought to be the largest underground city in Cappadocia until 2013, when construction workers found an even bigger one in the city of Nevşehir. Artifacts suggest that this second city is up to 5,000 years old. With more than 200 underground cities thought to exist in Cappadocia, it is likely that more will be discovered.

Online search terms: Cappadocia, Derinkuyu, Nevşehir, underground cities in Turkey

UNDERSTANDING THE READING *(page 127)*

40 MINS

A Understanding Main Ideas

Students are asked to identify the main idea of each paragraph.

- Have students complete the activity individually.
- Check answers as a class. Ask students where they found each main idea.

B Understanding Details

Students test their understanding of the details in the passage by completing the chart. The details expand on the main ideas in exercise **A**. Point out that some of the details are not found in the passage. For these, students should write "not given."

- Allow students time to complete the activity in pairs.
- Check answers as a class. Ask students where they found the answers.

C Critical Thinking: Understanding Analogies

The *Critical Thinking* box explains how analogies help readers visualize details more easily. In the passage, analogies are used to explain size. An area is compared to something that readers are familiar with to help them visualize how big, wide, or deep it is. Explain that a good analogy uses items that are common and easy to visualize, such as buses, buildings, or soccer fields. In exercise **C**, students are asked to spot analogies in two paragraphs and then identify what each analogy helps readers understand.

- Allow students time to complete the exercise in pairs.
- Check answers as a class. Ask students what items are used in each analogy and whether they can think of comparable analogies that would work better.

D Critical Thinking: Applying

Students create an analogy describing the age of the underground city in Nevşehir. Have students search online for ideas, if needed.

- Allow students time to complete the exercise in pairs.
- Discuss as a class. Elicit sample answers from students. Ask students how good each analogy is and why.

Ideas for... EXPANSION

Have students work in small groups to come up with various analogies to describe things famous for their size. Students can describe places, items, animals, or even people that are either very big or very small. Have each group present its answers and discuss how good each analogy is.

ANSWER KEY

UNDERSTANDING THE READING

A 1. F (Explanation: Only 30 of 200 underground cities have been discovered.)

2. C (Explanation: The paragraph lists many facilities found in the city; there are no records stating how old the city is.)

3. A (Explanation: A man knocked down one of the walls in his home and was surprised to find a hidden room carved into the stone.)

4. E (Explanation: *These artifacts suggest that the city is probably up to 5,000 years old.*)

5. B (Explanation: This city's large stone doors lead experts to believe that the city was built to protect its residents from enemies.)

6. D (Explanation: Derinkuyu was the largest known underground city in Cappadocia until 2013, when construction workers discovered a larger one.)

B Derinkuyu: a resident in the city; 60 meters deep; not given; 20,000 people; to protect residents (See Paragraphs B and C)

Below Nevşehir: construction workers; 110 meters deep; up to 5,000 years old; not given; to protect residents (See Paragraphs D and E)

C Paragraph B: depth (Explanation: …deep enough for a 20-story building)

Paragraph D: area; depth (Explanation: …an area big enough for 65 soccer fields; …deep enough to contain a 35-story building)

D Answers will vary. Possible answer: The city is as old as a wooly mammoth would be if it were still alive today!

20 MINS DEVELOPING READING SKILLS *(page 128)*

Reading Skill: Identifying Facts and Speculations

While a fact is true, a speculation is a guess or an idea that has not been proven. Scientists and explorers must often speculate because some of the evidence they find does not provide a definite answer. Common words indicating that a statement is speculation include *think*, *probably*, *possibly*, and *may*.

A Categorizing

The paragraph contains statements of both fact and speculation. Students should recognize the category for each statement and label the options accordingly.

- Allow students time to complete the task individually.
- Check answers as a class. Ask students for the words that indicate speculation.

B Categorizing

Students revisit the reading passage to determine whether the information described in each option is fact or speculation.

- Allow students time to complete the task individually.
- Check answers as a class. Ask students for the words that indicate speculation. Ask students whether they know other words, such as *perhaps* or *likely*, that also indicate speculation.

ANSWER KEY

DEVELOPING READING SKILLS

A 1. F (Explanation: He was born in Tangier, Morocco.)

2. F (Explanation: He left home at age 21.)

3. S (Explanation: He _may_ also have visited Beijing.)

4. F (Explanation: After traveling…over a period of 29 years)

5. S (Explanation: He _may_ have worked as a judge after he stopped traveling.)

6. S (Explanation: Battuta _probably_ died in 1368 or 1369.)

B 1. F (See Paragraph A: 1963)

2. F (See Paragraphs A and D: a resident; construction workers)

3. S (See Paragraphs C and E: There are no records of how old Derinkuyu is; artifacts _suggest_ that the city is _probably_ close to 5,000 years old.)

4. S (See Paragraph B and E: Experts _believe_ that both Derinkuyu and the city below Nevşehir were _probably_ built to keep people safe during times of war.)

5. S (See Paragraph F: Experts _believe_ there _may be_ more than 200.)

Video

VIEWING: THE LOST WORLD
(pages 129–130)

Overview of the Video

The Son Doong cave in Vietnam is one of the world's largest caves. In the video, a team of 40 cavers enters the cave with the goal of capturing 360-degree photos of the entire cave. The inside of the cave is huge and completely dark, so this is a big challenge. As the team journeys deeper into the cave, they encounter a sinkhole that allows sunlight into the cave. They are amazed by the size and beauty of the illuminated cave and describe how it feels as if they've gone back in time to the era of dinosaurs.

Online search terms: Son Doong cave, Martin Edström, Fly Through a Colossal Cave

BEFORE VIEWING

A Predicting

The photo shows just one illuminated section of the cave, but the entire cave is more than five kilometers long. Some caves are longer, but none are as wide or as high throughout. Some students will estimate the cave's size based on the photo, while others may notice that exercise **B** states that the cave is more than five kilometers long. Provide students with the information about the cave's size *after* they have created their analogies.

• Have students answer the question in pairs.

• Discuss as a class. Ask students to revise their analogies based on the new information you provided.

B Learning About the Topic

The paragraph prepares students for the video by providing background information about the discovery of Son Doong cave.

• Have students answer the questions individually.

• Check answers as a class.

C Vocabulary in Context

The sentences in the box contain three key vocabulary items that appear in the video. Students should use contextual clues to deduce the meanings of the words.

• Have students complete the exercise individually.

• Check answers as a class. Elicit sample sentences for each word.

BEFORE VIEWING

A Answers will vary. Possible answers: I think that the cave is as big as a 5-story shopping mall. / I think that it is deep and high enough to contain a football stadium. (Note: The cave is about the length of 50 football fields, or 100 Olympic-size swimming pools. From the video, students will learn that the cave is big enough to contain a whole city block of 40-story buildings.)

B 1. Vietnam

2. Natural (Explanation: The cave was created millions of years ago by river water.)

3. A team of British cavers

4. Answers will vary. Possible answers: unknown insect and fish species, crystals

C 1. vast

2. threat

3. heritage (Note: Students may be familiar with UNESCO World *Heritage* Sites, which are places that have been recognized for their cultural legacy.)

WHILE VIEWING

A ▶ Understanding Main Ideas

Have students read the items before you play the video.
- Have them complete the task while the video is playing.
- Check answers as a class. Ask students where they found the answers.

B ▶ Understanding Details

Have students read the questions and write any answers they recall from the first viewing before playing the video a second time.
- Have students complete the task while the video is playing.
- Check answers as a class. Have students explain their answers.

WHILE VIEWING

A c (Explanation: At the end of the video, we read that Edström wants to document the cave because it is under threat from tourism. He also says, "Places like this are part of our heritage and need to be preserved.")

B 1. a; **2.** b; **3.** b; **4.** a

AFTER VIEWING

A Reacting to the Video

Students are asked to consider whether they would enjoy exploring Son Doong as the cavers did in the video. For question **2**, ask students to brainstorm the possible effects of tourism.
- Allow time for students to answer the questions in pairs.
- Discuss as a class. For question **2**, elicit advantages and disadvantages from students, and list them on the board in two columns. Have the class vote to decide whether tourists should be allowed into Son Doong.

B Critical Thinking: Analyzing

Students are asked to recall and explain the analogy that appeared as a caption in the video. (00:25 *A city block of 40-story buildings could fit inside Son Doong Cave.*)
- Have students answer the questions in pairs. Play the video again, if necessary.
- Check answers as a class. Ask students to comment on whether the analogy made the size of the cave easy to visualize. Elicit some other possible analogies.

AFTER VIEWING

A Answers will vary. Possible answers:

1. I would like to visit Son Doong. It's beautiful inside, and I will be careful not to damage its special environment. / I don't want to visit the cave. I think only a few scientists should be allowed inside for research. We need to preserve it.

2. Advantages: Tourists will pay money to see the cave. We can use the money to protect the cave. / When tourists learn about how special places like this are, they will want to protect them more.

Disadvantages: Tourists will damage the cave's special ecosystem and endanger the species that live there. / Many tourists will probably litter and cause damage to the cave's environment.

B Answers will vary. Possible answer: The analogy described the size of the cave by stating that a city block of 40-story buildings could fit inside it.

Reading 2

30 MINS **PREPARING TO READ** *(page 131)*

A Building Vocabulary

The paragraph is about space exploration and life on other planets. It contains three key vocabulary items that appear in the passage. Students should use contextual clues to deduce the meanings of the words.
- Have students complete the exercise individually.
- Check answers as a class. Elicit sample sentences for each vocabulary item.

B Building Vocabulary

Students should first use dictionaries to check the definitions of the five words/phrases in blue before using them to complete the sentences.
- Have students complete the exercise individually.
- Check answers as a class. Elicit sample sentences for each vocabulary item.

See Vocabulary Extension 7B on page 209 of the Student Book for additional practice with collocations of the word run (run after, run into).

C Using Vocabulary

Students should use the new vocabulary items while answering the questions.
- Have students answer the questions in pairs.
- Discuss as a class. Elicit sample answers from students.

D Predicting

The photo is of a type of cave called a *blue hole*. The first paragraph explains that blue holes are unexplored, underground, and deep. Based on the photo, students should be able to infer that blue holes are huge underwater caves, and that it is very dark in there.
- Allow students time to skim the photo, title, caption, and first paragraph.
- Have them discuss their answers in pairs.
- Discuss as a class. Revisit this question after completing the reading.

ANSWER KEY

PREPARING TO READ

A 1. extremely (Note: The adverb *extremely* is an intensifier of descriptive words, or adjectives and other adverbs.)

 2. exist

 3. universe

B Answers will vary. Possible answers:

 1. challenging, risk (Note: The adjective *challenging* means difficult to do; the verb *risk* means to put something in a dangerous situation.)

 2. surface; run out (Note: *Running out* of something means using it until there is nothing left.)

 3. creatures (Note: The noun *creatures* generally refers to living things, but it is often used especially for unusual, scary, or fictional living things.)

C Answers will vary. Possible answers:

 1. Life definitely exists on other planets. I'm sure there's intelligent life out there somewhere in the vast universe! / I don't believe in aliens like we see in the movies, but maybe bacteria or algae exist on other planets.

 2. Cold climates are difficult to live in. It's extremely hard to grow crops and other plants in cold places. / I think living in desert areas must be extremely difficult. Deserts are usually dry and don't get much water.

D Answers will vary. Possible answers:

 Blue holes are probably located very deep underwater. They're probably very dark, too, when they're not lit up like they are in the photograph. It would be easy to get lost inside. Also, all those sharp edges must make exploration quite dangerous. (Note: The passage also mentions poisonous gases.)

🎧 **14** Have students read the passage individually, or play the audio and have students read along.

OVERVIEW OF THE READING

Blue holes are special caves that exist deep underwater. They have unique environments that scientists have not fully explored. The passage focuses on the blue holes in the Bahamas. Diving in blue holes is extremely dangerous. The passage describes the dangers and also the scientific reasons why divers risk their lives exploring them. The dark, oxygen-free environments offer scientists data not available elsewhere. For example, bacteria in blue holes are able to survive without oxygen. Studying them helps scientists understand how life could exist in similarly challenging conditions in space, such as on Jupiter's moon Europa.

Online search terms: blue holes in Bahamas, Dean's Blue Hole, astrobiologist Kevin Hand, remipede

UNDERSTANDING THE READING
(page 134)

A Understanding Purpose
Students are asked to identify the purpose of each paragraph.
- Allow students time to complete the activity individually.
- Check answers as a class. Ask students where they found the answers.

B Summarizing
Students complete a summary of the passage by choosing the correct options. Encourage them to answer from memory.
- Have students complete the summary individually.
- Check answers as a class. Ask students where they found the answers.

C Understanding Details
Students complete an infographic about blue holes using the details given in the passage.
- Allow students time to complete the activity in pairs.
- Check answers as a class. Ask students where they found the answers.

D Critical Thinking: Analyzing
Ask students to locate the relevant parts of the passage for each question and underline the words that indicate whether the information is a fact or a speculation before choosing their answers.
- Allow students time to complete the activity individually.
- Check answers as a class. Have students explain the answers.

Ideas for… **EXPANSION**

Have students search online for the *National Geographic Blue Holes Project* in pairs and view the photo gallery. Ask them to make speculations about what they see in the pictures.

Writing

OVERVIEW

Students learn how to write a paragraph describing something they want to do. The lesson starts by introducing expressions that convey interest and desire. It then teaches students how to strengthen reasons by introducing examples. In the *Writing Task*, students apply these lessons by writing about a place they would like to explore, providing reasons and examples. Students first brainstorm for ideas. They then select and organize their content before preparing a first draft. Finally, students improve their drafts and correct mistakes related to expression of interests and desires.

EXPLORING WRITTEN ENGLISH
(pages 135–137)

A Noticing

Student should pick up on the two categories of expressions that convey interest or desire: expressions ending with the word *to* (*would like to / would love to / want to*) and the one expression ending with *in* (*be interested in*). They should also notice the verb forms that go with each group. This exercise is to be done before going over the information in the *Language for Writing* box.

- Have students complete the task individually.
- Check answers as a class. Ask students what all of the sentences have in common, i.e., they express interest.

Language for Writing: Expressing Interests and Desires

The box lists four phrases that express an interest or desire to do something and describes how to use them correctly. Students should use the base form of a verb after the expressions ending with *to* and the *-ing* form of a verb after the expression *be interested in*. Highlight the use of the word *because* in the *Language for Writing* box. Students can use this word to give reasons for the things they want to do.

B Language for Writing

Students should use what they learned in the box to write their own sentences expressing interest or desire. Students first complete the chart with short answers. Next, they write complete sentences based on their notes in the chart.

- Allow students time to complete the exercise in pairs. Encourage partners to give each other feedback to help improve ideas and sentences.

- Check answers as a class. Elicit sample sentences from students.

> **ANSWER KEY**
>
> **EXPLORING WRITTEN ENGLISH**
>
> **A** **1.** discover; (would love to)
>
> **2.** study; learn (would like to; want to)
>
> **3.** visiting; see (would be interested in; want to)
>
> **4.** take; (want to)
>
> **5.** learning; visit (would be interested in; want to)
>
> **LANGUAGE FOR WRITING**
>
> **B** Answers will vary. Possible answers:
>
> **Things you want to do:** visit South America
>
> **Two reasons why:** see ancient sites; watch a soccer match live
>
> **Sentence:** I would like to visit South America because I am interested in exploring some of its ancient sites and watching a South American soccer match live.

Writing Skill: Introducing Examples

The *Writing Skill* box explains that examples can be used to expand on reasons. It builds on Unit 6, showing students more ways to introduce examples. It also explains the short form "e.g." and how it is not always appropriate to use it in formal writing. Lastly, remind students that they can use expressions like *also, in addition,* and *finally* to link their supporting ideas in this unit's writing task.

C Writing Skill

Students apply what they've learned in the *Writing Skill* box by completing the paragraph using the expressions in the box that introduce examples and order ideas.

- Have students work individually to complete the exercise.
- Check answers as a class.

D Writing Skill

Students are asked to write, in complete sentences, examples that expand on one of the things they listed in exercise **B**. A sample answer is provided in the Student Book. Students should link their reasons and introduce a suitable example for each reason using the expressions they have learned.

- Allow students time to complete the exercise in pairs.
- Discuss as a class. Elicit sample sentences from students. Give students feedback to help prepare them for the writing task.

WRITING SKILL

C **1.** First of all

2. A famous example

3. In addition

4. for instance

D Answers will vary. Possible answers:

I would like to visit South America because I want to see some of its historical sites. <u>A famous example is</u> Machu Picchu in Peru. I also would like to watch a South American soccer match live, <u>such as</u> the Boca Juniors against River Plate.

WRITING TASK *(page 138)*

A Brainstorming

Remind students that brainstorming is a useful first step for gathering ideas before writing. Read the *Goal* box aloud so that students are familiar with the writing task before brainstorming. Students should think of at least three places they want to explore. Have students look online for ideas, if needed. They need not list the reasons they want to go there. This will be covered in exercise **B**. Ideas should be briefly worded. They need not be listed in any order.

- Allow students time to complete the task individually.
- Have students discuss their ideas in pairs and give each other feedback.

B Planning

After brainstorming, students select their favorite place of the three and list in the outline three reasons they want to go there. Again, have students look online for ideas, if needed. Students should then list one or two examples for each reason. Remind students that complete sentences are not necessary. It is more important to focus on organizing their information.

- Allow students time to complete their outlines individually. Provide assistance as needed.

C First Draft

Have students write first drafts of their paragraphs based on their outlines.

- Allow students time to complete the task individually. Provide assistance as needed. Refrain from error correction at this point.

WRITING TASK

A Answers will vary. Possible answers: Southeast Asia, Europe, South America, Antarctica, New Zealand, New York City

B Answers will vary. Possible answers:

Topic Sentence: I would like to explore Africa.

Supporting Idea 1: See the wild animals

Detail: Wild cats in the savannah

Supporting Idea 2: See the monuments of Egypt

Detail: Pyramids of Giza

Supporting Idea 3: Visit its famous cities

Detail: Lagos in Nigeria

REVISING PRACTICE *(page 139)*

The *Revising Practice* box contains an exercise that demonstrates several ways students can improve their first drafts.

- Allow students time to analyze the two drafts and complete the exercise.
- Check answers as a class. Ask students to identify each change and explain how it makes the revised draft stronger.

D Revised Draft

Students should apply the revision techniques used in the *Revising Practice* box to their own drafts, where applicable.

- Explain to students that they will be using the questions as a guide for checking and improving their drafts.
- As a class, go over the questions carefully to make sure students understand them.
- Allow students time to revise their paragraphs.

EDITING PRACTICE

The *Editing Practice* box trains students to spot and correct common errors related to expressing interests and desires. As a class, go over the information in the box carefully to make sure students understand what to look out for.

- Allow students time to complete the exercise individually.
- Check answers as a class by asking students to read their corrected sentences aloud and explain the errors.

REVISING PRACTICE

d, c, b, a

EDITING PRACTICE

1. I would like <u>to</u> visit the Amazon rain forest because there are many different types of animals there.

2. I would love to <u>explore</u> New York City because it is full of interesting art and culture.

3. My brother and I are interested in <u>visiting</u> Russia because we want to learn more about Russian history.

4. My sister would like <u>to travel</u> to every continent because she loves to learn about different cultures.

5. My parents would like to go to Turkey one day because they want to <u>explore</u> the underground cities.

E Final Draft

Have students apply the skills taught in *Editing Practice* to their own revised drafts and check for any other errors.

- Allow students time to edit their drafts.
- Walk around and monitor students as they work. Provide assistance as needed.
- Collect their work once they have completed it.
- For the next class, show anonymous examples of good paragraphs and common errors.

UNIT REVIEW

Students can work in groups on this recap of the unit. For question **1**, encourage students to use the target words when appropriate. For questions **2** and **3**, encourage them to check the relevant pages of the unit for answers.

- Allow students time to answer the three questions in groups. For question **1**, get students to give a reason for their choice.
- Ask each group to present its answer for question **1**.

MUSIC WITH A MESSAGE

8

ACADEMIC TRACK

Arts / Music

ACADEMIC SKILLS

READING	Taking notes
WRITING	Planning a narrative paragraph
GRAMMAR	Using time expressions
CRITICAL THINKING	Interpreting idiomatic language

UNIT OVERVIEW

This unit is about musicians who are making a positive impact on the world. It shows how musicians can use their fame to make a difference by performing at benefit concerts, sharing their personal struggles, and speaking up about important issues.

- **READING 1:** Disabled street musicians from the Democratic Republic of the Congo inspire many people from around the world.

- **VIDEO:** The music festival WOMAD uses traditional music and dance to bring together people from around the world.

- **READING 2:** Three musicians from different parts of the world use their music and fame to support social causes.

Students draw on what they've read and watched to write a narrative paragraph about a musician they admire. The unit prepares them by introducing vocabulary to talk about music and social issues, explaining how to organize events in a timeline, and showing how to link these events using time expressions. It also teaches students how to take notes to summarize main ideas and details.

🕐 5 MINS THINK AND DISCUSS *(page 141)*

The photograph is of Ta'kaiya Blaney, a singer and environmental activist from Canada. While students may not be familiar with Blaney, the photo caption indicates that she's working to get more people to care about the environment. Details about her work appear later on page 156 of the Student Book.

- Have students study the picture, title, and caption.
- Discuss the photo as a class. Have students heard of Blaney? What does she do to spread her message?

Use the information from page 156 to give students some background.

- Discuss the two questions as a class. For question **2**, encourage students to share examples of environmentally conscious musicians. Remind students about Pharrell Williams's environmental activism, which they read about in Unit 4.

ANSWER KEY

THINK AND DISCUSS

Answers will vary. Possible answers:

1. I am a big fan of the K-pop band EXO. They are great dancers, and they're always so nice to their fans.

2. Musicians can use their fame to spread important messages, like Pharrell Williams who spreads the message about caring for the environment.

🕐 15 MINS EXPLORE THE THEME *(pages 142–143)*

The opening spread describes three benefit concerts that raised funds and awareness for social and environmental issues: Live 8, Oxjam, and Live Earth.

- Allow students time to study the spread and answer the questions individually.
- Check answers as a class.
- Elicit sample sentences from students for each of the blue words.

ANSWER KEY

EXPLORE THE THEME

A 1. Answers will vary. Possible answer: I once watched a benefit concert online. All the musicians spoke about protecting the environment before performing.

2. Answers will vary. Possible answer: Many musicians care about important issues and feel that they can use their fame and wealth to make a positive difference.

B audience; encourage; perform (Note: When we *encourage* someone, we usually suggest that they do something positive.)

Reading 1

30 MINS

PREPARING TO READ (page 144)

A Building Vocabulary

The paragraph is related to the theme of the reading passage. It describes two famous musicians who overcame their disabilities. It also contains three key vocabulary items that appear in the passage. Students should use contextual clues to deduce the meanings of the words.

- Have students complete the exercise individually.
- Check answers as a class. Elicit sample sentences for each vocabulary item.

B Building Vocabulary

Students should first use dictionaries to check the definitions of the four words in blue before using the words to complete the sentences.

- Have students complete the exercise individually.
- Check answers as a class. Elicit sample sentences for each vocabulary item.

See Vocabulary Extension 8A on page 210 of the Student Book for additional practice with the prefix dis- *(dislike, disadvantage).*

C Using Vocabulary

Students should use the new vocabulary items while answering the questions. Have students search online for ideas, if needed.

- Have students answer the questions in pairs.
- Discuss as a class. Elicit sample answers from students.

D Brainstorming

Students should think of as many reasons as possible before they select the best three. Offer students one or two examples before they begin.

- Allow students time to create their lists individually.
- Have them discuss their answers in pairs.
- Discuss as a class. Create a mind map on the board with their ideas. Ask students which reasons are most important to them personally.

E Predicting

The opening paragraph describes how two French filmmakers discovered the band Staff Benda Bilili. It mentions that most of the band's members are disabled. Students should make guesses about the types of challenges faced by disabled musicians such as those in Staff Benda Bilili. Remind students that *challenges* means *difficulties*.

- Allow students time to read the first paragraph and skim the title, photo, and caption.
- Have students discuss their answers in pairs.
- Discuss as a class. Revisit this question after completing the reading.

ANSWER KEY

PREPARING TO READ

A **1.** b

2. a

3. c (Note: While the word *disabled* is generally acceptable, synonyms such as *handicapped* or *crippled* have negative connotations and should not be used.)

B **1.** energetic

2. appearance

3. positive

4. documentary

C Answers will vary. Possible answers:

1. I once watched a documentary about the composer Mozart. Although he was very talented, I don't really enjoy classical music. / Hans Zimmer is a famous film composer. I really enjoyed what he wrote for the movie *Interstellar*.

2. The coffee shop down the street is a great place for live music. There are always new musicians performing there. / There are plenty of street performers near the farmer's market. Some of them are very talented.

D Answers will vary. Possible answers: Music unites people across cultures. / Music can spread positive messages. / Music helps people relax. / Music is an important part of other art forms, such as film and dance.

E Answers will vary. Possible answers: Disabled musicians might have a harder time carrying their instruments around with them. / They might have to figure out new ways to play an instrument, like the drummer of Def Leppard. (Note: While many members of Staff Benda Bilili are photographed performing in wheelchairs or on crutches, the main challenge described in the passage is that people often judge them by their appearances.)

15 Have students read the passage individually, or play the audio and have students read along.

OVERVIEW OF THE READING

The passage is about Staff Benda Bilili, a band from the Democratic Republic of the Congo. Most of its members are disabled, and the band's message is that you can be positive and strong, even when life is difficult. The band conveys this message through its lyrics and energetic performances. Its members see themselves as capable musicians and aspire not to be judged by their appearance. The passage describes how the group greatly impressed two French filmmakers who decided to make a documentary about them. The band traveled around the world, performing and inspiring people everywhere.

Online search terms: Staff Benda Bilili, Florent de la Tullaye and Renaud Barret

UNDERSTANDING THE READING
(page 147)

A Understanding Main Ideas

The passage contains two main sections. Students are asked to identify the main idea of each section.
• Have students complete the activity individually.
• Check answers as a class. Ask students why the other options are wrong.

B Understanding Details

Students test their understanding of the details in the passage by determining whether each statement is true or false.
• Allow students time to complete the task individually.
• Check answers as a class. Ask students where they found the answers. How would they make each false statement true?

C Critical Thinking: Inferring Meaning

Students should use contextual clues to deduce the meanings of three more words from the reading passage.
• Have students complete the task individually.
• Check answers as a class. Elicit sample sentences for each word. Ask students whether they know of any famous *choreographers* (Martha Graham) or if they've received *vaccinations* before (for chicken pox, measles, etc.).

D Critical Thinking: Interpreting Idiomatic Language

The *Critical Thinking* box explains that an idiomatic phrase has a meaning that is different from the literal meanings of the words in the expression. Students can use contextual clues to guess the meanings of idiomatic

phrases, just as they do for individual words. Ask whether students know any idioms before beginning the exercise, and provide a few examples, if necessary. For exercise **D**, ask students to look at the words around each expression for contextual clues and at the words in the expressions to see whether parts of it are familiar.
• Have students complete the activity individually.
• Check answers as a class. Elicit sample sentences for each idiom.

Ideas for… EXPANSION

Have students go online and watch performances by Staff Benda Bilili or a part of the documentary about the band. Then have students form groups and discuss their thoughts and impressions. Was the band's performance impressive or inspiring?

 DEVELOPING READING SKILLS *(page 148)*

Reading Skill: Taking Notes

The *Reading Skill* box explains that notes are a quick way to break down and summarize passages. Explain that notes are better in point form, not complete sentences. Students should paraphrase, or use their own words, to understand and remember the content better. Students should also use symbols and abbreviations. A few examples are given in the box. Also, explain that graphic organizers such as charts, Venn diagrams, mind maps, and timelines can help organize content better.

A Taking Notes

The chart breaks the passage up into paragraphs and their main ideas or topics. It also lists the supporting details for each main idea. It is an example of how a passage can be summarized in note form using a chart. Students should complete the chart by filling in the blanks with the correct information from the passage.

- Allow students time to complete the task individually.
- Check answers as a class. Highlight how some of the points make use of different words and abbreviations to paraphrase the passage. Also mention that bullet points make the notes easier to read.

B Applying

Students should use the chart in exercise **A** as a template for this exercise. Have students work in groups. Each group should choose a reading passage, reread it, and summarize it using a chart like the one in **A**. Remind students to write their notes in point form and to paraphrase and use symbols and abbreviations where suitable.

- Allow students time to complete the task in groups. Provide assistance as needed.
- Discuss as a class. Have each group present its chart. Ask students whether any of the points are too long or irrelevant. Can any of the words be shortened by using symbols or abbreviations?

ANSWER KEY

DEVELOPING READING SKILLS

A Paragraph B: composer

Paragraphs C and D: mission; appearances; positive

Paragraph E: the band members; rock musicians

Paragraph F: film/documentary; wars

Paragraph G: problems/challenges; polio

Paragraph H: hope

B Answers will vary.

Video

VIEWING: WORLD MUSIC
(pages 149–150)

Overview of the Video

For 30 years, WOMAD (World of Music, Arts, and Dance) festivals have brought together performers from around the world to share their traditional arts, music, and dance. The video starts with comments by British musician Peter Gabriel, who is one of the founders of the festival. It then focuses on the Italian group Spaccanapoli, who is making its first WOMAD appearance. Spaccanapoli's performance combines Italian folk rock and traditional dance. The video ends in Marcello Colasurdo's (the leader of Spaccanapoli) hometown of Naples, where music is very much a part of daily life.

Online search terms: WOMAD, Peter Gabriel, Marcello Colasurdo, Spaccanapoli

BEFORE VIEWING

A Predicting

The title of the passage should be enough for students to guess that the *W* and *M* in WOMAD stand for *World* and *Music*, but students will have to guess what the rest of the letters stand for. Ask students to think about words that are often associated with music. Note that the term *world music* often refers to a specific genre of music that mixes traditional or cultural music with more popular contemporary forms.

- Allow students time to study the title, photo, and caption.
- Discuss as a class. Ask students whether they have heard of WOMAD. Explain that it is a popular music festival, and go online together to look at information about it. Ask students whether they enjoy or think they would enjoy listening to world music.

B Learning About the Topic

The paragraph prepares students for the video by giving some background information about the WOMAD festival. Students should use the information to imagine what a WOMAD concert is like before answering the questions.

- Have students complete the task in pairs.
- Discuss as a class. Ask students who answer yes to question **2** to describe their concert experiences.

C Vocabulary in Context

This exercise introduces students to some of the key words used in the video. The paragraph also provides more background information about WOMAD.

- Have students complete the task individually.

- Check answers as a class. Elicit sample sentences for each word. Ask students why it is important to be *open-minded*.

BEFORE VIEWING

A   Answers will vary. Correct answer is: World of Music, Arts, and Dance

B   Answers will vary. Possible answers:

  1. WOMAD aims to introduce people to music, arts, and dance from around the world. / WOMAD's purpose is to bring cultures together and unite people through music, arts, and dance.

  2. Yes, I've been to music festivals that featured international artists. It was fun to listen to different kinds of music.

  3. You'll probably hear many more types of music at a WOMAD festival than you would at a rock or classical concert. WOMAD musicians probably also play many different types of instruments. The audiences will likely be as diverse as the music.

C 1. stunning

  2. traditional

  3. open-minded

WHILE VIEWING

A ▶ Categorizing

Have students read the items before you play the video.
- Have them complete the task while the video is playing.
- Check answers as a class. Ask students how Gabriel and Colasurdo are similar and how they are different. How is Colasurdo's music similar to rap music?

B ▶ Understanding Details

This exercise focuses on the later part of the video about Colasurdo's band, Spaccanapoli. Have students look at the concept map and write any answers they recall from the first viewing before playing the video a second time.
- Have students complete the task while the video is playing.
- Check answers as a class.

WHILE VIEWING

A 1. PG

  2. MC

  3. MC (Note: Colasurdo suggests that his music is like rap music because both forms of music draw deeply from the cultures from which they emerged.)

B 1. Italy

  2. tambourine

  3. first

  4. folk rock

  5. home town

AFTER VIEWING

A Reacting to the Video

Students are asked to imagine planning a WOMAD festival in their own country. Based on what they've learned about WOMAD, which local musicians would they invite to perform? Ask students to keep in mind the goals of WOMAD while answering.
- Allow students time to answer the question in groups.
- Discuss as a class. Come up with a full roster of musicians for the entire event.

> **Ideas for... EXPANSION**
>
> Have students form groups and play the role of a local band about to perform at WOMAD. Have each group come up with a band name and describe to the class the music and instruments they will be playing, the way Colasurdo did in the video. What can people expect from each group's WOMAD performance? What does each group hope that people will learn from watching them?

B Critical Thinking: Synthesizing

Students use information from both the *Video* and *Explore the Theme* sections to formulate their answers. Have students revisit the information on page 143 before answering the question.
- Allow students time to answer the question in pairs.
- Discuss as a class. Elicit sample answers from students. Are the goals of WOMAD as important as the goals of the three benefit concerts?

AFTER VIEWING

A   Answers will vary. (Note: Students should list local bands or musicians that have a traditional focus.)

B   Answers will vary. Possible answers: WOMAD is similar to Oxjam because they both have a global focus. / WOMAD is different from Live 8 because Live 8 happened just once in 2005. (Note: Although the primary goal of WOMAD isn't to raise money for charity, it does do this through the WOMAD Foundation.)

Reading 2

PREPARING TO READ *(page 151)*

30 MINS

A Building Vocabulary

In this exercise, the definitions of key words from the reading passage are provided. Students should use the definitions to help them complete the exercise.

- Have students complete the task individually.
- Check answers as a class. Elicit sample sentences for each vocabulary item.

See Vocabulary Extension 8B on page 210 of the Student Book for additional practice with the suffixes -ity and -ility (similarity, responsibility).

B Using Vocabulary

Students should use the new vocabulary items while answering the two questions. Give students one or two examples of social issues (the environment, education).

- Have students answer the questions in pairs.
- Discuss as a class. Elicit sample answers from students.

C Predicting

Each heading very loosely summarizes the cause championed by each of the three musicians. Have students skim through the passage for additional clues. They should spot words such as *child slavery* (Mraz); *prison camp, young Cambodians,* and *traditional music* (Chorn-Pond); *HIV* (Thabethe) The headings, together with these key words, should help students predict the answers.

- Allow students time to skim through the headings and passage for key words.
- Have students discuss their answers in pairs.
- Discuss as a class. Revisit this question after completing the reading.

ANSWER KEY

PREPARING TO READ

A
1. issue (Note: While *issue* is often used as a synonym for *problem*, it does not always have a negative connotation.)
2. treat (Note: When doctors or nurses *treat* someone, they provide medical care.)
3. responsibility; rescue
4. situation; bond
5. improve; escape

B Answers will vary. Possible answers: I think that poverty is a very important social issue. Some organizations, such as the Bill and Melinda Gates Foundation, are working to improve the situation by providing poor families with grants, for example.

C Answers will vary. Possible answers: Jason Mraz is using his fame to raise awareness of child slavery. Arn Chorn-Pond is helping his country recover from war by teaching young people how to play traditional Cambodian music. Zinhle Thabethe is using her music to give hope to patients with HIV/AIDS in South Africa.

🎧 16 Have students read the passage individually, or play the audio and have students read along.

OVERVIEW OF THE READING

The reading passage shows how musicians can affect the world positively by discussing three musicians who use their music to tackle humanitarian issues. American Jason Mraz uses his music and fame to raise awareness of child slavery. Cambodian Arn Chorn-Pond helps young Cambodians recover from the aftermath of war by teaching them traditional music and sharing his story of escape during the Khmer Rouge period. South African Zinhle Thabethe gives hope to patients with HIV by singing in a choir whose members are all HIV positive.

Online search terms: Jason Mraz, Free the Slaves, Arn Chorn-Pond, Zinhle Thabethe, Sinikithemba Choir

UNDERSTANDING THE READING

(page 154)

A Understanding Main Ideas

The chart is an incomplete summary of the main and supporting ideas in the reading passage. For exercise **A**, students match the main ideas to their paragraphs.

- Have students complete the task individually.
- Check answers as a class. Ask students where they found the answers.

B Taking Notes

Students should now fill in the blanks to complete each point in the chart. Remind them that they learned this skill in Reading 1. If necessary, review page 148 to go over the details of taking notes before students begin this exercise.

- Allow students time to complete the task individually.
- Check answers as a class. Ask students where they found the answers.

C Critical Thinking: Interpreting Idiomatic Language

Go over idiomatic language with students again. Have students locate the expression in the passage before using contextual clues to guess its meaning.

- Have students answer the question in pairs.
- Discuss as a class. Elicit sample sentences using the expression.

D Critical Thinking: Evaluating

Students are asked to compare the work of the three musicians and decide who does the most important work. Note that students' answers may be influenced by their own experiences or by the part of the world they are from.

- Have students answer the questions in pairs.
- Discuss as a class. Elicit sample answers from students. Encourage debate in the class, but remind students to be sensitive.

Ideas for… EXPANSION

Have students form pairs and choose a cause they care about. Ask them to formulate a plan to raise money and awareness for the cause with the help of a famous musician. Which musician would they work with? What will the musician do? Why is this musician suitable for their cause? Have students draft their plans and present them to the class.

Writing

OVERVIEW

In this lesson, students learn how to write a narrative paragraph that is ordered logically and sequentially. The lesson starts by teaching students how to use time expressions such as *during* and *before* to describe when an event happened. Students are then shown how to plan a narrative paragraph using a timeline. In the *Writing Task*, students apply these lessons by writing a narrative paragraph about the life of a musician they admire. Students first brainstorm key events in the musician's life. They then select and order these events in an outline before they draft their paragraphs, revise their drafts, and check for common errors with using time expressions.

EXPLORING WRITTEN ENGLISH
(pages 155–157)

A Noticing

Students should spot time expressions such as *in*, *during*, and *when* that help describe when an event happened. This exercise is to be done before going over the information in the *Language for Writing* box.
- Have students complete the task individually.
- Check answers as a class.

Language for Writing: Using Time Expressions

The *Writing Skill* box provides several examples of time expressions and explains how to use them. Time expressions can describe events in the past, present, or future; but this lesson focuses on past tense sentences. Highlight how a comma should be used when a time clause appears at the start of a sentence.

B Language for Writing

Students draw from what they've read and watched in the unit to complete the sentences using the correct time expressions. Point out that some items have more than one correct answer. Also explain that even though some time expressions fit grammatically, students should know from the context that they are not correct. Use question **1** as an example. (WOMAD was formed *in* 1982, not *before* or *after* 1982.)
- Have students complete the exercise individually.
- Check answers as a class. Ask students whether different answers are possible for each sentence.

C Language for Writing

Students use time expressions to write three sentences about their own lives. Students should write about three different events and use a different time expression in each sentence.
- Have them check answers in pairs.
- Discuss as a class. Elicit sample sentences from students.

See Grammar Reference on pages 219–223 of the Student Book for additional information on time expressions and time clauses.

ANSWER KEY

EXPLORING WRITTEN ENGLISH

A **1.** in
2. in
3. during
4. When

LANGUAGE FOR WRITING

B **1.** in
2. when / while
3. when / while
4. when / after
5. after
6. during
7. while / when

C Answers will vary. Possible answers: *When* I was three years old, my sister was born. / *Before* I started elementary school, we moved to a new city. / *During* my high school years, my team won the state basketball championship three times. / I spent a year traveling across Europe *after* high school. / *In* 2015, I started college.

Writing Skill: Planning a Narrative Paragraph

A *narrative* is a story with events that connect to each other, usually in a sequential and logical way. A person's life story is an example of a narrative. The *Writing Skill* box teaches students how to plan this type of narrative in three steps. First, make a list of life events using a timeline. Second, identify which events are significant and relevant. And third, create a topic sentence that ties the events together.

D Writing Skill

The paragraph describes the life of musician Ta'Kaiya Blaney, whose photo appears on the first page of the unit. However, some of the sentences are irrelevant. Students are asked to identify unimportant, unrelated sentences and cross them out.

- Allow students time to complete the task individually.
- Check answers as a class. Ask students to explain why the sentences should be removed. What is the paragraph's topic sentence? Do the deleted sentences relate to the main idea of the paragraph?

E Writing Skill

The paragraph contains key events in musician A.R. Rahman's life. They are not arranged in order. Students are asked to arrange information correctly and remove any irrelevant information.

- Allow students time to complete the task individually.
- Check answers as a class. Ask students to explain why the irrelevant sentence should be removed.

F Writing Skill

Point out that the list of events in exercise **E**, now arranged chronologically, is almost a complete narrative paragraph. All that's missing is a topic sentence. Students are asked to choose the most appropriate topic sentence out of the three options provided. Explain that in this type of narrative paragraph, the topic sentence is usually a general statement about the individual's life.

- Have students answer the question individually.
- Check answers as a class. Ask students why the other two options aren't suitable.

ANSWER KEY

WRITING SKILL

D Unnecessary sentences:
1. Climate change refers to a long-term change in global weather patterns.
2. The community has over 1,000 people.
3. The United Nations headquarters is in New York.
   (Note: The cut sentences do not relate to Blaney's life as a musician and environmental activist, which is the focus of the paragraph.)

E 1, 2, 3, 5, 7, 4, 8 (Cross out sentence number 6.)

F a

 WRITING TASK *(page 158)*

A Brainstorming

Remind students that brainstorming is a useful first step for gathering ideas before writing. Read the *Goal* box aloud so students are familiar with the writing task before brainstorming. Students should choose a musician or performer they admire and research them online. List as many major events in that person's life as possible.

Ideas should be briefly worded. They need not be listed in any order.

- Allow students time to complete the task individually.
- Have students discuss their ideas in pairs and give each other feedback.

B Planning

Students should now choose the best events they listed in **A** and arrange them in chronological order. Have them add details to each event and come up with a topic sentence that ties everything in the outline together. Remind students that complete sentences are not necessary. It is more important to focus on organizing their information.

- Allow students time to complete their outlines individually. Provide assistance as needed.

C First Draft

Have students write first drafts of their paragraphs based on their outlines.

- Allow students time to complete the task individually. Provide assistance as needed. Refrain from error correction at this point.

ANSWER KEY

WRITING TASK

A Answers will vary. Possible answers:

Musician / Performer: Zinhle Thabethe

Main life events / Key achievements: HIV diagnosis in 2002; Finally found a clinic that would treat her condition; Joined the Sinikithemba Choir and performed with other HIV-positive patients; Gave a TEDx Talk in 2010; Named as a National Geographic Emerging Explorer.

B Answers will vary. Possible answers:

Topic sentence: Zinhle Thabethe is a South African singer who is spreading hope to people living with HIV.

Event 1: Diagnosed with HIV in 2002.

Details: Thabethe initially struggled to find a doctor that could help her.

Event 2: Finally found a clinic that would treat her condition.

Details: Thabethe discovered the Sinikithemba Center, a clinic that had the medicine she needed.

Event 3: Joined the Sinikithemba Choir.

Details: The choir uses music to challenge stereotypes of HIV/AIDS patients.

Event 4: Gave a TEDx Talk in 2010.

Details: Thabethe shared what her organization is doing to help improve the issue of HIV/AIDS in Africa.

REVISING PRACTICE *(page 159)*

The *Revising Practice* box contains an exercise that demonstrates several ways students can improve their first drafts.

- Allow students time to analyze the two drafts and complete the exercise.
- Check answers as a class. Ask students to identify each change and explain how it makes the revised draft stronger.

D Revised Draft

Students should apply the revision techniques used in the *Revising Practice* box to their own drafts, where applicable.

- Explain to students that they will be using the questions as a guide for checking and improving their drafts.
- As a class, go over the questions carefully to make sure students understand them.
- Allow students time to revise their paragraphs.

EDITING PRACTICE

The *Editing Practice* box trains students to spot and correct common errors related to the use of time expressions. As a class, go over the information in the box carefully to make sure students understand what to look out for.

- Allow students time to complete the exercise individually.
- Check answers as a class by asking students to read their corrected sentences aloud and explain the errors.

E Final Draft

Have students apply the skills taught in *Editing Practice* to their own revised drafts and check for any other errors.

- Allow students time to work individually on editing their drafts.
- Walk around and monitor students as they work. Provide assistance as needed.
- Collect their work once they have completed it.
- For the next class, show anonymous examples of good paragraphs and common errors.

UNIT REVIEW

Students can work in groups on this recap of the unit. For question **1**, encourage students to use the target words when appropriate. For questions **2** and **3**, encourage them to check the relevant pages of the unit for answers.

- Allow students time to answer the three questions in groups. For question **1**, students should think about the actual impact each artist makes, and not which artist's cause is the most important.
- Ask each group to present its answer for question **1**.

ANSWER KEY

REVISING PRACTICE

a, c, b, d

EDITING PRACTICE

1. The violinist Itzhak Perlman became famous after he performed on TV <u>in</u> 1958.
2. In <u>1998, Beyoncé's</u> father quit his job to manage Destiny's Child.
3. Miles Davis moved to New York City to attend <u>Juilliard in</u> 1945.
4. After <u>Jay Z heard</u> Rihanna sing, he gave her a recording contract.
5. Lady Gaga was interested in acting <u>before she</u> decided to become a singer.
6. Adele composed her first song <u>when</u> she was 16 years old.

ANIMAL BEHAVIOR

ACADEMIC TRACK

Life Science / Anthropology

ACADEMIC SKILLS

READING   Recognizing noun clauses
WRITING   Writing a comparison paragraph
GRAMMAR   Making comparisons
CRITICAL THINKING   Inferring opinion

UNIT OVERVIEW

The unit looks at the behavior of animals—both domesticated and wild. It explores how some animals form close bonds with us and how others have a lot in common with us, such as the ability to use tools, a desire for fairness, and even a shared genetic heritage.

- **READING 1:** Celebrity dog trainer Cesar Millan shares his experience and knowledge of dog training.

- **VIDEO:** Photographic evidence reveals that gorillas make tools as humans do to solve everyday problems.

- **READING 2:** Studies show that capuchin monkeys dislike unfair treatment, shedding new light on our own desire for fairness.

Students draw on what they've read and watched to write a comparison paragraph about two animals. The unit prepares them by introducing vocabulary to talk about animal behavior, explaining noun clauses, teaching language for showing similarities and differences, and providing a structure for comparison paragraphs.

 THINK AND DISCUSS (page 161)

The photograph shows a mandrill monkey making an almost human-like expression. It is meant to get students thinking about how different animal behavior is from human behavior. The two questions also get students to discuss this. They focus on animal behavior and ability.

- Have students study the picture, title, and caption.
- Discuss the photo as a class. What emotion does the monkey look like it is expressing? Is the monkey really feeling that emotion?
- Discuss the questions as a class. For question **1**, ask students for examples of animals behaving like humans. For question **2**, ask students about animal abilities they would like to have.

EXPLORE THE THEME (pages 162–163)

The passage describes how similar humans are genetically to non-human primates, particularly chimpanzees. The passage also describes how dogs get along better with us than primates, even though they are genetically very different. The photo shows a friendly interaction between a chimpanzee and scientist Dr. Jane Goodall. Dr. Goodall is recognized for her groundbreaking work on chimpanzee behavior.

- Allow students time to study the spread and answer the questions individually.
- Check answers as a class. For question **3**, ask students which animal is *closest* to us. Explain that *close* can imply two things: *affection* or *similarity*.
- Elicit sample sentences from students for each of the blue words.

Reading 1

30 MINS

PREPARING TO READ *(page 164)*

A Building Vocabulary

The paragraph is related to the reading passage. It is about dog training and its origins. The paragraph contains four key vocabulary items that appear in the passage. Students should use contextual clues to deduce the meanings of the words.

- Have students complete the exercise individually.
- Check answers as a class. Elicit sample sentences for each vocabulary item.

B Building Vocabulary

Students should first use dictionaries to check the definitions of the three words in blue before using the words to complete the sentences.

- Have students complete the exercise individually.
- Check answers as a class. Elicit sample sentences for each vocabulary item.

See Vocabulary Extension 9A on page 211 of the Student Book for additional practice with the suffixes -er and -or (composer, instructor).

C Using Vocabulary

Students should use the new vocabulary items while answering the question. Explain that some personality traits are often regarded as important *soft skills*. Give students one or two examples (the ability to work well with others, grit, an eye for detail).

- Have students answer the question in pairs.
- Discuss as a class. Elicit sample answers from students.

D Skimming

Students are asked to skim through the interview questions only, not the entire passage. The interview questions are *italicized*. Since this reading passage is an interview, the questions will give a clear idea of what topics are discussed.

- Allow students time to skim through the title and the interview questions.
- Discuss as a class. Revisit this activity after completing the reading.

ANSWER KEY

PREPARING TO READ

A 1. profession

 2. trainer

 3. approach (Note: The verb form of *approach* means to move toward.)

 4. work out (Note: Another common meaning of this expression is to exercise.)

B 1. powerful (Note: A *powerful* person can be physically strong like a weightlifter or exert a strong influence over others like a president.)

 2. angry

 3. confused (Note: People and animals get *confused*, while situations get *confusing*.)

C Answers will vary. Possible answers: A dog trainer needs to be confident, because dogs can sense when a trainer is nervous or unsure. / A dog trainer should be able to read a dog's body language, because dogs can't communicate using words or signs.

D Answers will vary. Correct answers:

 1, 3, 4 (Explanation: *Why do people like certain kinds of dogs? / What are the lessons we learn from dogs? / So which animals behave better—humans or dogs?*)

🎧 **17** Have students read the passage individually, or play the audio and have students read along.

OVERVIEW OF THE READING

The passage is an interview with celebrity dog trainer and author Cesar Millan, whose National Geographic TV show has made him world-famous for his skills with dogs. In a personal interview, Millan discusses his experience with dogs and dog training: how dogs think, feel, and act, and the common mistakes human owners often make with dogs. Cesar Millan's job is as much about training owners as it is about training dogs. Millan says that although people choose dogs that they feel reflect their own personalities, owners should treat their pets as pets, not as humans.

Online search terms: Cesar Millan, Dog Whisperer, Cesar 911

 **UNDERSTANDING THE READING** *(page 167)*

A Understanding Main Ideas

Students are asked to choose the statements that reflect the main ideas Cesar Millan expresses in the interview.

- Have students complete the task individually.
- Check answers as a class. Ask students where they found their answers. Ask students why the other options are wrong.

B Understanding Details

Students choose the correct options based on their understanding of the details in the passage.

- Allow students time to complete the task individually.
- Check answers as a class. Ask students where they found their answers.

> **Ideas for... EXPANSION**
>
> Ask students whether they have dogs or other pets. Do students agree with Cesar Millan that pets are reflections of their owners' personalities? Should pets be treated as pets and not as people?

C Understanding Pronoun Reference

The word *they* in each of the sentences refers to something different. Students need to identify who or what *they* refers to in each case. Encourage students to complete the activity without referring to the passage.

- Have students complete the task individually.
- Check answers as a class. Ask students where they found their answers.

D Critical Thinking: Inferring Opinion

The *Critical Thinking* box describes the skill of inference, or understanding what is said indirectly. In the passage, Millan's answers are often short, so knowing how to make inferences is an important skill here. Students can read more into his answers by looking at context and attitude. In exercise **D**, students practice this by matching each inference with the corresponding sentence from exercise **C**.

- Allow students time to complete the task individually.
- Check answers as a class. Have students explain the answers.
- What other inferences can be made from Millan's comments? For example, what do his comments about Beverly Hills and Harvard degrees show what he thinks about the relationship between being rich/highly educated and training a dog?

UNDERSTANDING THE READING

A 2, 4 (Explanation: For option 2, the first paragraph states that Millan helps dogs and dog owners deal with their problems. / For option 4, in response to the fifth question, Millan says, "I see the dog, and I know who you are.")

B 1. treating dogs like people (Explanation: *We humanize dogs. We hold conversations with them as if they were people. . .*)

2. want from (Explanation: *It's about what they want from another human but can't get, so they get it from a dog.*)

3. similar to (Explanation: *I see the dog, and I know who you are. It's a mirror.*)

4. firm (Explanation: *You don't ask a dog if it would like to go for a walk. You put on the leash and go.*)

5. honesty (Explanation: *Also honesty . . . [and] integrity.*)

C 1. His clients

2. His parents (Explanation: The sentence is a response to the question "How did your parents feel about your choice of profession?")

3. Dogs (Explanation: The sentence is a response to the question "What are the lessons we learn from dogs?") (Note: To *stab someone in the back* is to betray or hurt someone who trusts you.)

D a. 2 (Explanation: Millan's parents don't think that dog training is important work and don't understand why people pay for his services.)

b. 3 (Explanation: The question asks what humans can learn from dogs. Millan answers that dogs don't stab people in the back, suggesting that humans do.)

c. 1 (Explanation: Even though training a dog is easy for him, a lot of people struggle with it.)

 **DEVELOPING READING SKILLS** *(page 168)*

Reading Skill: Recognizing Noun Clauses

The *Reading Skill* box introduces students to noun clauses. A noun clause is a group of words that functions as a noun.

The box demonstrates this, using three steps: identifying a subordinating conjunction (*who, what, how, why,* and *that*), checking that the clause contains a subject and verb, and replacing the noun clause with a noun/pronoun.

A Recognizing Noun Clauses

Students complete the sentences by choosing the correct noun clauses from the passage. Ask students to try to complete the exercise without looking at the passage.

- Have students complete the task individually.
- Check answers as a class. Ask students where they found the answers. Have them identify the subject and the verb in each noun clause.

B Recognizing Noun Clauses

Students must identify the noun clauses in the paragraph before answering the three questions. All of the noun clauses begin with subordinating conjunctions (*who, what, why, how,* etc.).

- Allow students time to complete the task individually.
- Have students discuss their answers in pairs.
- Check answers as a class.

Video

VIEWING: GORILLA TOOLMAKERS *(pages 169–170)*

40 MINS

Overview of the Video

Field researchers Thomas Breuer and Emma Stokes discovered that gorillas in northern Congo could think through problems and use tools to solve them. Breuer describes how he photographed a gorilla using a stick to test the depth of a river before crossing it. While gorillas in captivity have been known to use sticks to find food, the use of tools by wild gorillas was a new discovery. Scientists used to believe that the ability to use tools was a unique human ability, but research has since shown that many animals are able to use tools creatively to solve problems. That gorillas are also able to do this reveals that they are more like us than we had previously thought.

Online search terms: Thomas Breuer, Emma Stokes, Wildlife Conservation Society, gorilla toolmaking

BEFORE VIEWING

A Predicting

The word *Toolmakers* in the title should stand out and draw attention to the gorilla's use of a branch in the photo to find food. This is described in the caption. Students should predict that the ability to use items as tools is one trait gorillas share with humans. Encourage students to come up with their own ideas as well.

- Have students answer the question in pairs.
- Discuss as a class. Elicit sample answers from students. Ask students why the ability to make tools is considered special.

B Learning About the Topic

The paragraph prepares students for the video by providing background information about the use of tools by animals. The paragraph lists two reasons why animals use tools: to find food and to build nests. Encourage students to think beyond the paragraph and to list reasons of their own. Have them search online for ideas.

- Allow students time to complete the exercise in pairs.
- Discuss as a class. Elicit sample answers from students. Ask students to name other animals they know that use tools.

C Vocabulary in Context

This exercise introduces students to some of the key words and phrases used in the video. The sentences also give more information about the use of tools by humans and animals.

- Have students complete the task individually.
- Check answers as a class. Elicit sample sentences for each word.

BEFORE VIEWING

A   Answers will vary. Possible answers: Both humans and gorillas know how to use tools. / Humans and gorillas are similar genetically. / Humans and gorillas have very similar hands, with four fingers and a thumb on each.

B   Answers will vary. Possible answers:

1. to hunt
2. to build homes and nests
3. to swat away insects
4. for protection against predators

C 1. stick

2. invent
3. evidence (Note: *Evidence* is an important part of scientific research and police investigations.)
4. think through

WHILE VIEWING

A ▶ Understanding Main Ideas

Have students read the items before you play the video.
- Have them complete the task while the video is playing.
- Check answers as a class. Discuss why the other statements are wrong.

B ▶ Understanding Details

Have students read the questions and write any answers they recall from the first viewing before playing the video a second time.
- Have students complete the task while the video is playing.
- Check answers as a class.

WHILE VIEWING

A   b

B 1. the same way humans do

2. check the depth of the water
3. find food
4. using a new tool

AFTER VIEWING

A Reacting to the Video

Students are asked to compare and contrast gorilla and human behavior. Limit students to the topic discussed in the video: toolmaking.
- Allow students time to answer the question in pairs.
- Discuss as a class. Elicit sample answers from students.

B Critical Thinking: Reflecting

Students are asked to think about how new findings about animals, such as the ones described in the video and in this unit, benefit humans.
- Allow students time to answer the questions in pairs.
- Discuss as a class. Elicit sample answers from students.

AFTER VIEWING

A   Answers will vary. Possible answers:

Like humans, gorillas are able to use tools to solve problems. However, unlike humans, gorillas are unable to shape or design tools from scratch. Instead, they use what's readily available.

B   Answers will vary. Possible answers: We are able to better understand our own behavior when we study similar behavior in animals. / When we learn how similar animals are to us, we will be more interested in protecting them and the natural environments that they live in.

Reading 2

PREPARING TO READ (page 171)

30 MINS

A Building Vocabulary

In this exercise, the definitions of key words from the reading passage are provided. Students should use the definitions to help them complete the exercise.

- Have students complete the task individually.
- Check answers as a class. Elicit sample sentences for each vocabulary item.

See Vocabulary Extension 9B on page 211 of the Student Book for additional practice with homonyms (words with the same spelling and pronunciation but different meanings).

B Using Vocabulary

Students should use the new vocabulary items while answering the two questions. For question **1**, give students an example of unfair treatment.

- Have students take turns asking and answering the questions in pairs.
- Discuss as a class. Elicit sample answers from students. For question **2**, do students wish they had responded differently?

C Predicting

The title states clearly that the passage is about whether monkeys have feelings. The first subheading suggests that monkeys are able to show a sense of fairness, while the second subheading shows that monkeys can have feelings of kindness. Students should infer that the paragraphs that follow each subheading present evidence to back up this claim.

- Allow students time to skim through the title, headings, photos, and captions.
- Have students discuss their answers in pairs.
- Discuss as a class. Revisit this question after completing the reading.

🎧 **18** Have students read the passage individually, or play the audio and have students read along.

OVERVIEW OF THE READING

The reading passage talks about two different studies. In the first, pairs of capuchin monkeys were rewarded unequally for performing similar tasks. One monkey received a better reward, which caused the other to react angrily. The result confirmed that monkeys understand and dislike unfair treatment, leading researchers to question whether fairness is hardwired in both animals and humans. The second study shows that kindness in macaques can be affected by the hormone oxytocin. Macaques that received the hormone were more likely to share their food with other macaques, suggesting that kindness, fairness, and cooperation may be inherent biological traits. The capuchin study was conducted by Sarah Brosnan, and the macaque study was done by a team at Duke University.

Online search terms: Sarah Brosnan, Moral Behavior in Animals, monkeys and fairness, capuchin fairness experiment, macaques oxytocin experiment

UNDERSTANDING THE READING *(page 174)*

A Understanding Main Ideas

Students match main ideas from the first study to the correct categories.
- Have students complete the exercise individually.
- Check answers as a class. Discuss where each main idea can be found. Ask students to imagine how a sense of fairness would benefit capuchins. Highlight their cooperative nature mentioned in Paragraph B.

B Summarizing

Students fill in the blanks to complete a summary of the second study.
- Allow students time to work individually.
- Check answers as a class. Ask students where they found the answers.

C Understanding Pronoun Reference

Students must first find the sentences in the passage before using context to identify the nouns that the pronouns are referring to.
- Have students complete the exercise individually.
- Have them check answers in pairs.
- Check answers as a class. Ask students to replace the underlined pronouns with their answers and determine whether the sentences make sense.

D Critical Thinking: Applying

Get students to imagine themselves as human subjects in the capuchin experiment. How do they think they and other people would respond? How could the experiment be modified to suit humans better? For example, would knowing that they were in an experiment affect results? What tasks and rewards would be better for people?
- Have students answer the questions in pairs.
- Discuss as a class. Elicit sample answers from students and list them on the board.

Writing

OVERVIEW

The lesson takes students through the steps of writing a comparison paragraph. It starts by introducing language for talking about similarities and differences before teaching students how to structure a comparison paragraph. In the *Writing Task*, students apply these lessons by writing a paragraph comparing the behavior of two different animals. They begin with a brainstorming exercise before they select and organize the similarities and differences in an outline. They then write a first draft, which they revise before finally checking for common mistakes with language for making comparisons.

EXPLORING WRITTEN ENGLISH (pages 175–177)

A Noticing

Students should notice the words that describe similarities (*both*, *like*) and differences (*unlike*, *however*) while completing the exercise. This exercise is to be done before going over the information in the *Language for Writing* box.

- Have students complete the exercise individually.
- Check answers as a class. Ask students how they arrived at their answers.
- Use the underlined words students identified as a lead-in to the *Language for Writing* box.

Language for Writing: Making Comparisons

The *Language for Writing* box introduces phrases for making comparisons. When making a comparison, students should describe both similarities and differences. The box teaches three ways to do each. Point out that the expressions taught in the box will be central to the writing task later.

B Language for Writing

Students practice making comparisons by using the words in parentheses to combine the sentences. Point out that there may be more than one way to combine some of the sentences.

- Have students complete the activity individually.
- Check answers as a class. Ask whether any students joined the sentences differently.

C Language for Writing

Venn diagrams present similarities and differences in a way that is instantly clear. Students should write full sentences about the information in the chart, using words

for making comparisons. Point out that students do not need to combine their sentences to form a paragraph.

- Allow students time to complete the activity individually.
- Have them check answers in pairs. Ask each pair to come up with different ways to convey each point.
- Check answers as a class. Elicit sample sentences from students.

See Grammar Reference on pages 219–223 of the Student Book for additional information on words and phrases for making comparisons.

Writing Skill: Writing a Comparison Paragraph

The *Writing Skill* box explains that comparison paragraphs typically focus entirely on similarities or entirely on differences (although this may not always be the case in advanced writing). It presents three rules for organizing a comparison paragraph. First, include a general topic sentence that states the things being compared. Second, use a broad description of each similarity or difference as a supporting idea. Third, use examples as details to expand on each supporting idea. The box provides a breakdown of this structure. Explain that comparison paragraphs are sometimes called compare/contrast paragraphs. To compare two things usually means to look at both similarities and differences. To contrast them is to look only at their differences. Students need to pay close attention to the instructions when tackling these types of activities.

D Sequencing

Students are asked to form a comparison paragraph about two types of big cats by arranging the sentences in order. The paragraph follows the structure described in the *Writing Skill* box.
- Have students complete the task individually.
- Check answers as a class. Ask students to identify the topic sentence, supporting ideas, and details. Point out that the paragraph only describes similarities.

E Writing a Topic Sentence

The paragraph in **E** is missing a topic sentence, and students are asked to come up with one. This should be a general statement about the two things being compared that ties together all three supporting ideas.
- Allow students time to complete the activity individually.
- Have students share their answers in pairs.
- Discuss as a class. Ask students what the three supporting ideas are and what they have in common. (They all point out differences.) Elicit sample topic sentences.

F Writing Skill

The words in bold from the paragraph in **E** help structure a comparison paragraph. Students are asked to identify synonyms for each word.
- Have students complete the activity individually.
- Check answers as a class. Ask students about the functions of the bold words.

WRITING TASK (page 178)

A Brainstorming

Remind students that brainstorming is a useful first step for gathering ideas before writing. Read the *Goal* box aloud so students are familiar with the writing task before brainstorming. Students should think of animals with notable behavioral traits. Gorillas are given as an example, so students should choose something different. Suggest that it is more interesting to compare two animals that appear similar on the surface but behave differently or vice versa. Allow students to search online for ideas, if possible. Ideas should be briefly worded. They need not be listed in any order.
- Allow students time to complete the task individually.
- Have students discuss their ideas in pairs and give each other feedback.

B Planning

Students must first decide which two animals they want to compare and whether they want to focus on similarities or differences. Next, they need to organize their ideas in an outline. They should use broad descriptions of each similarity or difference as supporting ideas and specific examples as details. Lastly, they should write their ideas for an appropriate topic sentence. Remind students that complete sentences are not necessary. It is more important to focus on organizing their information.
- Allow students time to complete their outlines individually. Provide assistance as needed.

C First Draft

Have students write first drafts of their paragraphs based on their outlines. Remind them to use words for making comparisons when appropriate.
- Allow students time to complete the task individually. Provide assistance as needed. Refrain from error correction at this point.

WRITING TASK

A Answers will vary. Possible answers:

Crows: solve puzzles; fashion tools; recognize faces

Parrots: friendly; use sticks to get food; solve puzzles; recognize faces

B Answers will vary. Possible answers:

Topic sentence: Parrots may look friendly, and crows may appear fierce, but both are incredibly smart animals.

Supporting Idea 1: Both can use tools.

Detail: Both are known to use sticks to get food.

Supporting Idea 2: They can solve puzzles.

Detail: They are able to improvise clever solutions in lab experiments.

Supporting Idea 3: They can recognize faces.

Detail: Crows recognize specific people as threats. Parrots recognize their owners.

REVISING PRACTICE *(page 179)*

The *Revising Practice* box contains an exercise that demonstrates several ways students can improve their first drafts.

- Allow students time to analyze the two drafts and complete the exercise.
- Check answers as a class. Ask students to identify each change and explain how it makes the revised draft stronger.

D Revised Draft

Students should apply the revision techniques used in the *Revising Practice* box to their own drafts, where applicable.

- Explain to students that they will be using the questions as a guide for checking and improving their drafts.
- As a class, go over the questions carefully to make sure students understand them.
- Allow students time to revise their paragraphs.

EDITING PRACTICE

The *Editing Practice* box trains students to spot and correct common errors with language for making comparisons. As a class, go over the information in the box carefully to make sure students understand what to look out for.

- Allow students time to complete the exercise individually.
- Check answers as a class by asking students to read their corrected sentences aloud and explain the errors.

REVISING PRACTICE

c, a, b, d

EDITING PRACTICE

1. Like <u>humans,</u> chimpanzees use tools to solve problems.
2. Both female capuchins and humans <u>value</u> fairness.
3. Some chimpanzees use tools in zoos. <u>In</u> contrast, gorillas rarely use tools in captivity.
4. Unlike <u>cats,</u> dogs need a lot of attention from their owners.
5. Some dog trainers believe in punishing bad behavior. <u>However, other</u> trainers believe in rewarding good behavior.
6. Both Basenjis and Australian Terriers <u>make</u> good pets for children.
7. Scientists often use monkeys in behavioral studies. <u>Similarly, rats</u> are useful for scientific research on behavior.
8. Like <u>children, dogs</u> need a lot of training and attention.

E Final Draft

Have students apply the skills taught in *Editing Practice* to their own revised drafts and check for any other errors.

- Allow students time to edit their drafts.
- Walk around and monitor students as they work. Provide assistance as needed.
- Collect their work once they have completed it.
- For the next class, show anonymous examples of good paragraphs and common errors.

UNIT REVIEW

Students can work in groups on this recap of the unit. For question **1**, encourage students to use the target words when appropriate. For questions **2** and **3**, encourage them to check the relevant pages of the unit for answers.

- Allow students time to answer the three questions in groups. For question **1**, encourage students to draw from both the examples in the book and their own ideas.
- Ask each group to present its answer for question **1**.

THE POWER OF IMAGES

UNIT OVERVIEW

The theme of this unit is images and how they affect us. The unit explains what makes an image powerful and demonstrates how striking images can leave lasting impressions. Students will also read comments by experienced photographers about the power of images and photography.

- **READING 1:** An award-winning photographer shares his thoughts on what makes a great photograph.

- **VIDEO:** Young refugees learn how to document their lives through photography at a National Geographic Photo Camp.

- **READING 2:** A wildlife photographer describes, through words and photographs, a surprising encounter he had with a leopard seal.

Students draw on what they've read and watched to write an opinion paragraph about a photograph they like. The unit prepares them to do this by introducing vocabulary to describe photographs and teaching students how to describe spatial relationships and emotions. It then breaks down and explains the structure of a typical opinion paragraph. Students also learn to differentiate between subordinating conjunctions that show time relationships and contrast.

 THINK AND DISCUSS (page 181)

This photograph of Jamaican sprinter Usain Bolt shows him looking back and smiling with a considerable lead over his opponents. While the photo shows how incredibly quick Bolt is, it also shows his confidence.

- Have students study the picture, title, and captions.
- Discuss the photo as a class. Have students seen it before? What is impressive about the photo?
- Discuss the two questions as a class. For question **1**, ask students whether they think the photo of Bolt is powerful and why. For question **2**, encourage students to share photos they've taken themselves.

ANSWER KEY

THINK AND DISCUSS

Answers will vary. Possible answers:

1. A powerful photograph should inspire people, like this photograph of Usain Bolt. It makes me feel as if anything is possible.

2. I saw a photo of an ant colony in a magazine once. It was so amazing to see the ants up close, working tirelessly as a team.

 EXPLORE THE THEME (pages 182–183)

The opening spread describes National Geographic photographer Annie Griffiths's views on taking great photographs.

- Allow students time to study the spread and answer the questions individually.
- Check answers as a class. Ask students to identify which of Griffiths's elements appear in each photo. Which photo do they like the best?
- Elicit sample sentences from students for each of the blue words.

ANSWER KEY

EXPLORE THE THEME

A 1. Composition, moment, and light.

2. Answers will vary. Possible answers: color, motion, wonder, uniqueness

B element; quality; emotion

Ideas for... EXPANSION

Have students search the Internet for some of Annie Griffiths's photographs. Then ask them to discuss which ones they like and why. Encourage them to use the vocabulary and information from the spread to comment on light, composition, and moment.

Reading 1

PREPARING TO READ (page 184)

A Building Vocabulary

The sentences in the box contain seven key vocabulary items that appear in the reading passage. Students should use contextual clues to deduce the meanings of the words.

- Have students complete the exercise individually.
- Check answers as a class. Elicit sample sentences for each vocabulary item.

See Vocabulary Extension 10A on page 212 of the Student Book for additional practice with words containing vis *and* vid *(visual, video).*

B Using Vocabulary

Students should use the new vocabulary items while answering the two questions.

- Have students answer the questions in pairs.
- Discuss as a class. Elicit sample answers from students.

C Brainstorming

Students should come up with three emotions and examples of photographs for each emotion. Ideas should be brief. Offer students one or two examples before they begin. Allow students to search online for photographs.

- Have students complete the task in pairs.
- Discuss as a class. Elicit sample answers from students. List the different emotions on the board, and encourage students to add the emotions to their vocabulary notebooks.

D Predicting

The three main photos are the ones described in the passage: the gorilla, the Mbuti girl, and the Vietnamese girl on the swing. Students are asked what each depicts. Follow up by asking what they have in common and how they connect us, as the title suggests. Each of the photographs is an example of a good photograph, based on the criteria given by photojournalist David Griffin. According to Griffin, photos like these resemble vivid flashbulb memories of powerful emotional events, which we all have. Do not explain this to students; instead, lead the discussion toward how each image makes students feel.

- Allow students time to study the photos.
- Have students discuss their answers in pairs.
- Discuss as a class. Revisit this question after completing the reading.

PREPARING TO READ

A **1.** suddenly

  2. ceremony (Note: A *ceremony* is usually to celebrate something, such as a wedding or graduation.)

  3. point out

  4. visual

  5. remind

  6. capture (Note: While the verb *capture* is used here in reference to images, it is also commonly used to refer to taking something as one's own, often by force, such as an army *capturing* enemy territory.)

  7. scene (Note: The word *scene* can also describe a view that is not in a picture, such as a landscape you are looking at.)

B Answers will vary. Possible answers:

  1. People often take photos of important events in their lives, such as weddings or graduation ceremonies. / My favorite moments to photograph and capture are everyday moments, when people are doing ordinary things and don't notice the camera.

  2. I remind myself of important things by setting an alarm on my cell phone. / I remind myself of important things by making notes in my diary.

C Answers will vary. Possible answers: joy, sadness, grief, awe, fear, wonder

D Answers will vary. Possible answers: It looks like the men are carrying a dead gorilla to its burial place. / The young girl is probably thinking about something. I don't think she knows that she is being photographed. / A little girl is playing on a swing while her mother works nearby.

19 Have students read the passage individually, or play the audio and have students read along.

OVERVIEW OF THE READING

The passage is based on a TED Talk given by David Griffin, called *How Photography Connects Us*. Griffin talks about what makes a picture great. He starts by describing flashbulb memories, or the way we remember and visualize powerful personal events in our minds. He explains that good photographs are like flashbulb memories, which is why we are able to connect emotionally with them. Griffin also explains that the best photographers capture images that tell a story.

Online search terms: David Griffin TED, flashbulb memory

UNDERSTANDING THE READING *(page 189)*

A Understanding Main Ideas

Students test their understanding of what makes a great photo, according to Griffin.

- Allow students time to complete the activity individually.
- Check answers as a class. Ask students where they found the main ideas. Do students have any flashbulb memories of their own?

B Understanding Details

Students test their understanding of the details in the article by matching the descriptions to the three images in the passage. Point out that some details apply to more than one photo.

- Have students complete the task individually.
- Check answers as a class. Ask students where they found their answers.

C Critical Thinking: Evaluating Using Criteria

The *Critical Thinking* box explains how we can evaluate things better by using criteria. Students should use Griffiths's three elements in *Explore the Theme* to evaluate the photos in the reading passage. Allow students time to review the elements, and ask them to think of reasons for each of their ratings.

- Have students complete the chart individually.
- Discuss as a class. Elicit sample answers from students. Have students add up their ratings for each photo. Does the photo they like best have the highest total score? How reliable are Griffiths's criteria?

D Critical Thinking: Analyzing

Students think about which photos in the Student Book elicited emotional responses like the ones Griffin described in the passage. Allow students time to go through the photos in the book before beginning the exercise.

- Allow students time to answer the questions in pairs.
- Discuss as a class. Elicit sample answers from students.

UNDERSTANDING THE READING

A Answers will vary. Possible answers:

1. Griffin describes his son's near drowning. (See Paragraph A)
2. A flashbulb memory is a clear and detailed memory of a powerful and emotional event. (See Paragraph B)
3. It captures an emotional scene the same way the mind remembers an emotional event. (See Paragraph C)

B **1.** a, b, f;   **2.** a, d, e;   **3.** c, d

C Answers will vary.

D Answers will vary. Possible answers:

Description: Usain Bolt winning his race by a big margin

Emotions it communicates: excitement, awe

Description: The woman looking at her baby

Emotions it communicates: love, pride

Ideas for… EXPANSION

Have students decide on an environmental problem that needs to be addressed, such as global warming or deforestation. Then ask students to imagine that they are coming up with an ad campaign to help tackle the issue. Have students form small groups and go online to look for a suitable photograph to use in their ad. Their photo should tell a story and have a strong emotional connection. Have each group explain its photo choice before voting as a class on the most powerful photo.

DEVELOPING READING SKILLS *(page 190)*

Reading Skill: Identifying Subordinating Conjunctions

The *Reading Skill* box explains that subordinating conjunctions (also called dependent conjunctions) show the relationship between clauses. Time and contrast are two ways that clauses can be related to each other. The box introduces the conjunctions *after, before, until, while,* and *as* to show time relationships and the conjunctions *although, even though, though,* and *while* to show contrast. Highlight to students that *while* can be used to show both time relationships and contrast. Also point out that a comma is included in between the independent clause and the subordinating clause if the latter is showing a contrast.

A Identifying Conjunctions

Students are asked to determine whether the subordinating conjunction in each sentence introduces a time relationship or contrast.
- Have students complete the exercise individually.
- Check answers as a class. Have students explain the answers.

B Analyzing

Students are asked to find three sentences from the reading passage that contain subordinating conjunctions and to determine whether each shows a time relationship or contrast. The paragraphs containing the conjunctions are provided in the exercise.
- Allow students time to complete the task individually.
- Check answers as a class. Have students explain their answers.

C Applying

Students are asked to write sentences about two photographs from the reading passage. They should use subordinating conjunctions in their sentences to show either a time relationship or contrast.
- Allow students time to complete the task individually.
- Discuss as a class. Elicit sample answers from students.

ANSWER KEY

DEVELOPING READING SKILLS

A 1. T
2. C (Note: The word *while* indicates contrast between the words *professional* and *amateur*, which are antonyms.)
3. T
4. T
5. C

B 1. Time: *As Griffin ran to help his son, time seemed to slow down.*
2. Time: *He photographed a woman in the Vietnamese countryside working while her daughter played on a swing.*
3. Contrast: *Although many of the most powerful images are taken by professional photographers, Griffin points out that amateur photographers can also capture a special moment.*

C Answers will vary. Possible answers:
After the gorilla was killed, the village held a funeral ceremony for him. / Even though it was the Mbuti boy's ceremony, the photographer focused his camera on the girl. / The girl played on the swing while her mother worked hard.

Video

VIEWING: PHOTO CAMP
(pages 191–192)

Overview of the Video

Sixty young refugees in Uganda attend a National Geographic Photo Camp where they learn the basics of photography from highly acclaimed National Geographic photographers. The photo camp aims to help these young people gain a new skill and see their lives through a different lens. The photographers encourage the refugees to tell their stories through pictures and to photograph things that are important to them. They teach the young people, many of whom have never used a camera before, how to compose a shot and see their surroundings in new ways. At the end of the camp, the refugees exhibit their photos. They leave with a certificate and a practical new skill, as well as the means to document their lives in a way that the world can appreciate and understand.

Online search terms: National Geographic photo camp, Reza Deghati, Ed Kashi, Chris Rainier, Neo Ntsoma

BEFORE VIEWING

A Predicting

The photo shows the participants of a photo camp in the Bahamas. This is not the same photo camp shown in the video. The participants are young, and they look like regular students. However, exercise **B** elaborates that the attendees of National Geographic Photo Camps are young people who live in difficult situations. All of the children are holding the same type of camera, which suggests that they are there to learn about photography.
- Allow students time to study the title, photo, and caption.
- Discuss as a class. How can learning photography help young people who grow up in challenging situations?

B Learning About the Topic

The paragraph prepares students for the video by giving them background information about National Geographic Photo Camps. Note that the paragraph answers the *Predicting* questions from exercise **A**.
- Have students complete the task individually.
- Check answers as a class. Ask students where they found their answers.

C Vocabulary in Context

This exercise introduces students to some of the key words used in the video. The paragraph also gives background information about Reza Deghati, one of the instructors shown in the video.

- Have students complete the task individually.
- Check answers as a class. Elicit sample sentences for each word.

WHILE VIEWING

A ▶ Understanding Main Ideas

Have students read the items before you play the video.
- Have them complete the task while the video is playing.
- Check answers as a class. Discuss why the other statements are wrong.

B ▶ Understanding Details

Have students read the items and write any answers they recall from the first viewing before playing the video a second time.
- Have students complete the task while the video is playing.
- Check answers as a class. Ask students how to make each false statement true.

AFTER VIEWING

A Reacting to the Video

Students are asked to interpret an idiomatic expression for the first question and to apply the concept of Photo Camp to other groups of people that might benefit from it in the second question.
- Allow students time to answer the questions individually.
- Have them discuss their answers in pairs.
- Discuss as a class. Elicit sample answers from students. For question **2**, ask what the goals of the photo camp are and who would benefit the most from it.

B Critical Thinking: Applying

Students should choose one of the groups they identified in question **2** of exercise **A** and come up with a photo camp plan for that group. Encourage students to come up with more details than just the location and the goals.
- Allow students time to complete the task in pairs.
- Discuss as a class. Elicit sample answers from students.

> **Ideas for… EXPANSION**
>
> Have students work in pairs or small groups to come up with a script for a radio commercial for their photo camps. Each commercial should explain what happens in the camp and how it will benefit participants. It should also ask for donations in support of the project. Ask each group to present its ad, and have the class vote on the ad that sounds the most promising.

Reading 2

PREPARING TO READ (page 193)

A Building Vocabulary

In this exercise, the definitions of key words from the reading passage are provided. Students should use the definitions to help them complete the exercise.

- Have students complete the task individually.
- Check answers as a class. Elicit sample sentences for each vocabulary item.

See Vocabulary Extension 10B on page 212 of the Student Book for additional practice with changing verbs to adjectives ending in -ed and -ing (interested, disappointing).

B Using Vocabulary

Students should use the new vocabulary items while answering the two questions.

- Have students answer the questions in pairs.
- Discuss as a class. Elicit sample answers from students. Ask students to explain the difference between feeling *nervous* and feeling *frightened*.

C Predicting

The three photographs are all of leopard seals, as specified in one of the captions. From this alone, students will likely guess that the purpose of Nicklen's trip to Antarctica was to research these animals. This is confirmed at the end of Paragraph B, which states that he wanted to find out whether leopard seals were as dangerous as some people think.

- Allow students time to skim the first two paragraphs, title, photos, and captions.
- Have students discuss their answers in pairs.
- Discuss as a class. Revisit this activity after completing the reading.

🎧 20   Have students read the passage individually, or play the audio and have students read along.

OVERVIEW OF THE READING

The reading passage is about a close encounter between wildlife photographer Paul Nicklen and a giant leopard seal in the waters of Antarctica. It starts by describing leopard seals as fierce predators. Nicklen wanted to find out whether this is true. Are leopard seals as dangerous as they seem? The passage continues with a personal account of the close encounter. Nicklen recounts his first frightening moments with the animal and goes on to describe how he eventually bonded with the seal, which at one point tried feeding Nicklen penguins it had caught. Nicklen formed a surprising connection with the seal and learned that animals don't always behave in ways you expect. The passage is based on Nicklen's TED Talk *Animal Tales from Icy Wonderlands*.

Online search terms: Paul Nicklen leopard seal, Animal Tales from Icy Wonderlands, Face-to-Face with a Leopard Seal

UNDERSTANDING THE READING *(page 196)*

A Understanding Main Ideas

Students choose the title that best sums up the main idea of the passage.

- Have students complete the task individually.
- Check answers as a class. Ask students how they arrived at the answer.

B Sequencing

Students are asked to arrange the events of Nicklen's seal encounter in order. The events appear in Paragraphs C to G.

- Allow students time to complete the task individually.
- Check answers as a class. Ask students where they found the answers.

C Paraphrasing

Students practice paraphrasing by retelling Nicklen's story in their own words. Remind students that they covered paraphrasing in Unit 8 while learning how to take notes. Also remind students to use subordinating conjunctions to show time relationships or contrast. Start by having students retell Nicklen's story to each other. After that, have them write down paraphrased summaries in pairs. Encourage students to work from memory.

- Allow students time to complete the task in pairs.
- Discuss as a class. Elicit sample answers from students. Have them read their summaries aloud, and ask for volunteers to retell the story without a script.

D Critical Thinking: Evaluating Using Criteria

Students apply Griffiths's criteria in *Explore the Theme* to the three photos in the reading passage. Students should decide which element stands out the most in each photo. Go over her criteria with students again, if necessary.

- Allow students time to complete the task in pairs.
- Discuss as a class. Elicit sample answers from students. Ask students to give reasons for their opinions. Point out that there is no right or wrong opinion, because people can feel differently about each photo.

Ideas for… EXPANSION

Have students watch Nicklen's TED Talk *Animal Tales from Icy Wonderlands* (10:50 onward) to hear more about Nicklen's unforgettable encounter with the leopard seal and to look at more of his photographs. Then ask students to work in the same pairs they were in for exercise **C** and add more sentences with subordinating conjunctions to the paraphrased summaries they wrote.

ANSWER KEY

UNDERSTANDING THE READING

A c (Explanation: The passage's main point is that he formed an incredible bond with the leopard seal.)

B f, b, a, e, d, c, h, g

C Answers will vary. Possible answer:

Nicklen went to Antarctica to find out whether leopard seals were dangerous. <u>While</u> he was on his boat, a leopard seal swam nearby. <u>Although</u> he was afraid, Nicklen got into the water with the seal. <u>When</u> he entered the water, the seal swam right up to him. <u>Even though</u> it tried to bite Nicklen and his camera, Nicklen remained calm. He soon realized the seal was trying to befriend him. It tried to feed him penguins and even protected him from other seals. <u>After</u> swimming in the water with the seal for four days, Nicklen learned that animals may sometimes behave in unexpected ways.

D Answers will vary. Possible answers:

1. Light: The light makes every frightening detail in the leopard seal's mouth very clear.

2. Moment: The timing of the close-up shot captures perfectly how strange it must have felt when the leopard seal first brought Nicklen a penguin.

3. Composition: It's easy to appreciate how big the leopard seal is because of how close it is to the diver.

Writing

OVERVIEW

In this section, students write an opinion paragraph about a photograph. The lesson starts by introducing expressions used for describing spatial relationships to help students describe where things are located in an image. Students then learn how to describe emotions: to state how they feel about what they see. Finally, they learn about the structure of a typical opinion paragraph: state your opinion as the topic sentence; list reasons as supporting ideas; provide details to explain each reason. In the *Writing Task*, students apply these lessons by writing a paragraph explaining why they think a photograph is good. Students begin by brainstorming for reasons before selecting the best ones and organizing them in an outline. Students then draft their paragraphs, improve their drafts, and correct common mistakes with describing spatial relationships.

EXPLORING WRITTEN ENGLISH *(pages 197–199)*

Language for Writing: Describing Spatial Relationships

The first *Language for Writing* box teaches students expressions for describing spatial relationships, or where things are relative to each other. These expressions will be useful in the *Writing Task*. Many of the expressions might already be familiar to students, but draw special attention to the expressions describing *foreground* and *background*. Use the photo of the Mbuti girl on page 187 to explain what these concepts mean. Point out that even though the girl is in the background, the photographer has chosen to make her the focus of the picture. Typically, photographs focus on things in the foreground.

A Analyzing

Students are asked to analyze the photograph of a mother with her child in a park on page 183 and to choose the correct expression to describe where things are in the photo. If possible, project the photo for students to refer to while completing the exercise.

- Allow students time to complete the activity individually.
- Check answers as a class. For questions **2**, **4**, and **7**, explain that the descriptions *right* and *left* are based on the viewers' perspective, and not the subjects in the photo.

Language for Writing: Describing Emotions

The second *Language for Writing* box focuses on the verbs we use to describe emotions. When describing what we think people in an image are feeling, or how we think a scene feels, we use verbs such as *seem, feel,* and *look* to show that these are opinions and not certainties. When we talk about our own emotions and how we feel when looking at an image, we use verbs such as *make* and *remind*. Explain that when we describe how an image makes us feel, the image is the subject and we are the object of the sentence. The image does something to us: It causes us to feel a certain way or think of certain things.

B Language for Writing

Students unscramble the words to form sentences that describe emotions. Some of the sentences describe how people in a photo look and feel, while others describe the emotions of someone looking at an image.

- Allow students time to complete the activity individually.
- Check answers as a class.

C Language for Writing

Students practice describing both spatial relationships and emotions in this exercise. Ask students to choose a photo from the unit and describe the key elements in it. Then have them write about how it makes them feel and explain these feelings by stating what the elements in the photograph remind them of.

- Allow students time to make notes about an image individually.
- Have them share their sentences in pairs. Ask students to try to guess the photo their partner is describing.
- Discuss as a class. Elicit sample answers from students. Ask other students whether they feel the same way about the photos.

EXPLORING WRITTEN ENGLISH

LANGUAGE FOR WRITING

A 1. background
2. to the right of
3. front
4. right
5. in front of
6. behind
7. left
8. foreground

B 1. The boy seems happy and relaxed.
2. The dead gorilla makes me feel sad and angry.
3. The clouds look like a house.
4. This image reminds people of environmental problems.
5. The young girl makes us think of a famous sculpture.

C Answers will vary. Possible answers:

Description: In the foreground, a girl plays on a swing. Behind her in the background, her mother is hard at work making rope.

How it makes me feel: The girl on the swing makes me feel happy. She reminds me of how much fun it was to play on swings as a child. The hardworking mother makes me feel grateful. She reminds me of my own mother, who also works hard to support me.

Writing Skill: Writing an Opinion Paragraph

The *Writing Skill* box explains the structure of a typical opinion paragraph. The topic sentence states the opinion, while the supporting ideas and details provide reasons and examples or explanations. As covered in *Describing Emotions*, the emotions a photo depicts are good examples of reasons that can be used as supporting ideas in an opinion paragraph about a photo. Stating what the photo reminds us of is a good way to elaborate on these reasons. Alternatively, students can also use the technical qualities of a photo as reasons to support their opinions.

D Writing Skill

Students are asked to identify the different parts of an opinion paragraph.

- Have students complete the task individually.
- Check answers as a class. List the steps on the board in the correct order so that students can see the paragraph's skeleton clearly. Explain that a concluding sentence is a great way to avoid ending a paragraph awkwardly.

WRITING SKILL

D a, c, e, d, f, b

WRITING TASK *(page 200)*

A Brainstorming

Remind students that brainstorming is a useful first step for gathering ideas before writing. Read the *Goal* box aloud so students will be familiar with the writing task before brainstorming. Students should select three photos. Encourage students to use their own photos, if possible. Have them work in pairs and discuss what makes each photo good and write notes of their reasons. Ideas should be briefly worded. They need not be listed in any order.

- Allow students time to choose their photos individually.
- Have students discuss their photos in pairs and offer feedback to each other.

B Planning

Students choose one photo to write about and come up with a topic sentence that summarizes their opinion. They then list three reasons as supporting ideas and add details to expand each supporting idea. Remind students that complete sentences are not necessary. It is more important to focus on organizing their information.

- Allow students time to complete their outlines individually. Provide assistance as needed.

C First Draft

Have students write first drafts of their paragraphs based on their outlines.

- Allow students time to complete the task individually. Provide assistance as needed. Refrain from error correction at this point.

WRITING TASK

A Answers will vary. Possible answers:

Photo 1: Sea lions playing in the water

Reasons: Lighting; Composition; Motion

Photo 2: Usain Bolt competing at the Olympics

Reasons: Motion; Composition; Tells a story

B Answers will vary. Possible answer:

Topic Sentence: I think that the photo of Usain Bolt competing at the Olympics is a really good photo.

Supporting Idea 1: The interesting expression on Bolt's face

Detail: Perfectly captures Bolt's emotion during his race

Supporting Idea 2: The slight blurring of the image

Detail: Makes the race look very fast paced and intense

REVISING PRACTICE   (page 201)

The *Revising Practice* box contains an exercise that demonstrates several ways students can improve their first drafts. The two paragraphs are about the photo of a mother and her baby in a park on page 183 of the Student Book.

- Allow students time to analyze the two drafts and complete the exercise.
- Check answers as a class. Ask students to identify each change and explain how it makes the revised draft stronger.

D Revised Draft

Students should apply the revision techniques used in the *Revising Practice* box to their own drafts, where applicable.

- Explain to students that they will be using the questions as a guide for checking and improving their drafts.
- As a class, go over the questions carefully to make sure students understand them.
- Allow students time to revise their paragraphs.

EDITING PRACTICE

The *Editing Practice* box trains students to spot and correct common errors related to expressions used for describing spatial relationships. As a class, go over the information in the box carefully to make sure students understand what to look out for.

- Allow students time to complete the exercise individually.
- Check answers as a class by asking students to read their corrected sentences aloud and explain the errors.

REVISING PRACTICE

b, a, c, e, d

EDITING PRACTICE

1. Next <u>to</u> the boys is a large group of elephants.
2. In this photo, a mother is sitting between her son <u>and</u> her daughter.
3. A young girl in a pink coat is standing <u>behind her</u> brother.
4. <u>In</u> the middle of the scene, there is a small yellow fish.
5. <u>In</u> the foreground, we see a small dog in a green sweater.
6. There is a large <u>tree behind</u> the little boy.
7. There is a baby <u>to</u> the right of her mother.
8. The children are <u>beside the</u> water buffaloes.

E Final Draft

Have students apply the skills taught in *Editing Practice* to their own revised drafts and check for any other errors.

- Allow students time to edit their drafts.
- Walk around and monitor students as they work. Provide assistance as needed.
- Collect their work once they have completed it.
- For the next class, show examples of good paragraphs and common errors. Check that students who have written about their personal photos are OK with sharing them with the class.

UNIT REVIEW

Students can work in groups on this recap of the unit. For question **1**, encourage students to use the target words when appropriate. For questions **2** and **3**, encourage them to check the relevant pages of the unit for answers.

- Allow students time to answer the three questions in groups. For question **1**, try to form groups based on which pictures students like.
- Ask each group to present its answer for question **1**. As a class, vote for the best photo in the unit.

VIDEO TRANSCRIPTS

UNIT 1   A Global Conversation

Monesjia Hi. I am Monesjia. This is my partner, Lulu. Today, we're going to take Kazakhstan on our journey. Let's get started.

Orazalina Anel Hello, everybody. My name is Orazalina Anel.

Smagulova Anel And my name is Smagulova Anel.

Orazalina Anel Today, we want to show you how we shop.

Monesjia As you can see, down in north Philly, it's fall. The leaves are red, brown, green.

Kazakh student We love winter, and also love play snow balls.

Monesjia Here we are taking you to our playground. We come to this playground mostly every day. It's called Penrose. It's on 12 Susquehanna.

Orazalina Anel It's our bus stop. There… we wait our bus. There it's a little lake. There are people do ice fishing.

Passerby See you later.

Monesjia Thank you!

French student I am going to do a beat box demonstration. OK, now I would like to ask you a question. Is there something about you guys that could amaze others?

Philadelphia boys Bonjour, Paris!

Brandon Hello, my name is Brandon, aka DB Beez.

Steven Yo, what's up, my name's Steven, aka DB Steve-o.

Jalen Hey, my name's Jalen, aka, DB Play.

Tymir My name's Tymir, aka Darth Vader.

Nasir My name's Nasir Coates, aka DB Kid.

Jalen We are a dance group in Philadelphia. We practice 24/7, cause we have to, like everything has to be on point, like …

Brandon Crisp.

Man Are you ready?

French student This was very good!

Sannii Crespina-Flores Puberty is purity. Being a teen is a team. They find that there are so many similarities. They're more connected, and more alike than they are separate. It's an exchange of possibilities.

Various students Is there graffiti in Kazakhstan?

What are your activities in Africa?

Do you like living in Nigeria?

Are your foods spicy or sweet?

Are there rich people there?

Do you have any like gold or diamond crowns?

Can you describe the block you grew up on?

When you reach 18, are you going to live alone?

When I fall asleep, I do dream about waking up in other countries.

I would like to go to Germany. I want to travel to Brazil.

I would like to visit Morocco.

America is like, a paradise.

Have you ever been on a plane before?

I feel that like, everybody should be able to go all over the world. The world is as big or as small as you make it.

UNIT 2   A School for Change

Shabana I spent a great chunk of my childhood under the Taliban regime. There were literally no schools for girls. My parents have always made it known to me and to my siblings that education is their number one priority for us.

Six percent of women in Afghanistan have a college degree. To be a part of that small minority, I feel extremely lucky and privileged. But at the same time, how did I get to be so lucky? Maybe there was a reason. I realized that I needed to become an educator.

I'm the president and co-founder of SOLA, School of Leadership Afghanistan. It's the first girls' boarding school in Afghanistan. Their education has a real purpose. Not just for them to have a good job, good income, but their education is also for them to serve their country. To be responsible global citizens.

Teacher Exactly, 9 times 4.

Shabana The process of empowerment has to be initiated from within. We create a safe space for these girls to be able to grow into their confident selves. There you go, see, you can all do it. Do you want to try?

Various students If I can't be a doctor, I want to be a teacher of science.

I want to be an explorer.

I want to be so many things, but it's really hard to decide.

I want to be a doctor and a teacher.

I want to prove that girls can do everything.

Teacher Okay, what subject? History?

Shabana They all come here to learn to become the future leaders of Afghanistan. The solution to problems in Afghanistan have to come from Afghans. When you educate a girl, you educate her family, her community, her society, and our world at large.

UNIT 3 Who Do You Trust?

Jason In this next experiment, we're going to show you the faces of different candidates from various local elections. We've paired up some of the winners with some of the losers. Something tells me somehow you're gonna be able to pick the winner, just by looking at them.

Ready? See if you can tell which of these candidates won their election.

Got it? Now here's the real result.

Now, how about these two?

Here's the winner…

What about these two?

And the winner is…

So how did you do? Did you pick most of the winners? The majority of the people we surveyed did.

Jason So how did you pick those winners? How could you know based on nothing more than seeing their faces for just a few seconds? Bulgarian perception specialist Alex Todorov of Princeton University found the answer in a groundbreaking 2007 experiment.

Todorov A very rapid glance is sufficient to predict about 70 percent of the election outcomes.

Jason 70 percent of the time, we can predict the winners of elections, based on their faces alone. Pretty incredible—but what is it about these winners that persuaded your brain to vote for them? It's not just the clothes, the background, or even the smile. The answer has to do with two specific qualities you saw in their facial structure.

Todorov In our studies we found that candidates who look more competent and more trustworthy were more likely to be elected in office.

Jason Competence and trustworthiness. You may find it hard to believe your brain can make such complex social assessments based on a face alone. But it can. Give it a shot.

Which one of these faces looks the most trustworthy?

This one? Or this one? What about this one? Made your choice?

If you chose face one, you're with 85 percent of the people we surveyed.

Although our judgments of someone else's character aren't necessarily accurate, they happen in the blink of an eye. Todorov's study revealed your brain can literally decide if it trusts someone within a tenth of a second of seeing his or her face.

Todorov As the face becomes more feminine, it becomes more trustworthy. It also becomes looking much happier. As it becomes more masculine, it becomes less trustworthy.

Jason Wanna see how your brain's snap judgments about trustworthiness play out in the real world? I'm taking a few more of these photos to a New Jersey mall to see if volunteers can call elections based only on some photos.

Who do you think looks more trustworthy?

Which one's your choice? Let's see what some of these folks say.

Man 1 I would have to go with this guy.

Man 2 I'm going to go with him.

Jason Vote for me, vote for me.

Man 3 I have to go with the one on the right.

Woman I'm just going by my gut.

Man 4 He's got a nicer face.

Man 2 He looks more comfortable. He looks approachable.

Jason As it turns out, he beat this guy in a local election.

Man 1 First impressions.

Jason Your impression was the same as the majority voter. You didn't know anything about their policies, you didn't know what they were running on and yet you basically knew who the winner was.

Man 3 That's really interesting.

Jason Right?

Amazingly, time and again these people chose the actual winners based just on their looks.

We like to think we make informed decisions when it comes to politics. But at a subtle level, we're all being persuaded by first impressions whether or not we even realize it.

UNIT 4 Trash People

Narrator When garbage collectors take our trash away, we usually don't think about it again. But a German artist, HA Schult, is transforming trash into something very familiar. And he's giving us the chance to think about trash in a new way.

Schult I made a thousand sculptures from garbage. And these sculptures are people like us.

Narrator HA sculpted the trash people out of materials from a German landfill, but you can find these materials anywhere in the world.

Schult The garbage today is an international garbage. We know that the garbage of China comes to Europe, the garbage of Europe goes to Russia, the Russian garbage goes to South Africa. We are in a time where the world may be garbage. We're on the garbage planet.

Narrator HA shows his art around the world. He wants people to see that garbage is a problem everywhere.

Schult Everywhere, in Giza, in Egypt, or in China, on the Great Wall, people have known that I show the problems of our time. And these problems are in every country, the same.

Narrator HA first set up 1,000 trash people in Xanten, Germany. Then they went to Red Square in Moscow, along the Great Wall of China, to the foot of the Matterhorn in Switzerland, and then to the Egyptian pyramids. Now the trash people are at National Geographic headquarters in Washington, D.C.

HA watches as workers set the trash people up, but he lets the sculptures tell their own story to the visitors.

Schult I think the answer to the future will come from the children of today. And the children are traveling also around the world now because we are living in a global village.

Narrator What does our garbage say about us? The trash people don't talk, but they clearly have a lot to say.

UNIT 5   Images of Greenland

Narrator In 2014, photographer Matthieu Paley traveled to Greenland to learn about the lifestyle and diet of the Inuit. Here, he talks about his experience.

Paley I decided after much research to go to Greenland. And I went to the eastern part of Greenland, which is less inhabited. And so I went to this place called Isortoq. And they eat only meat traditionally.

This is Isortoq. That's the whole of it. And it took me two flights and two helicopter rides to get there. I had contacted a family before, so when I arrived I was met by this family. And I spent ten days sleeping there in the living room. I was staying with Bengt—he's there in green—and Dina (standing up). And they're hunters. They go hunting a few times a week. They're active hunters still.

Narrator Soon after his arrival, Paley joined his hosts on a seal hunt. He took photos of the experience.

Paley So we go out. We drive out and they are looking for what they like, mostly seal. So she's looking at this environment, looking for little black spots to pop up.

Narrator For four days, they searched for seals, but weren't able to find any. However, they did catch several birds called ptarmigan. Paley took photos as Dina prepared the birds for dinner, but it wasn't really what he was looking for. For Paley, it didn't feel like a real Arctic experience.

Paley So I said, I asked Dina cooking, and I said, "Do you have like anything like more Arctic, like whale?" And she's like, "Yeah, I got plenty of whale meat." So she popped out this beautiful bag of you know… I'm like "nope, not working." But then I still needed to get some hunting scene, you know something that is telling where you see… And then I hear about this other hunter, who would often go hunting on canoe, because you can approach animals much more quietly. And I said, "Hey, bring me on."

Ah yes… I saw something here, I think, a little black spot. Yeah yeah! Magnus, Magnus, here!

That means "head of a seal." Sign language. And so, that's right there. You see—that's the head of a seal. It comes out, for about 10–20 seconds, and then it would just dive back in. So you have to be quick, you have to be close. Also, you need quiet sea, because if there's waves, you can't see the head.

Narrator That day, they were able to see the seals, but again weren't able to catch any. But one day, when Paley was hunting with Bengt and Dina, they finally caught one. They brought the seal back to the village.

Hunting and preparing meat has been part of life for the Inuit for thousands of years. Although the Inuit are starting to adapt to the modern world, in some ways their lifestyle remains the same as it has been for generations. And so the Inuit continue to survive in this remote place at the top of the world.

UNIT 6   Living on Mars

Narrator Scientists around the world are interested in exploring Mars. Over the past 30 years, there have been dozens of unmanned missions to the red planet. However, traveling to Mars is not easy: about two-thirds of these missions were failures.

Because missions to Mars are dangerous and expensive, plans for a manned mission to Mars have been delayed for decades. The international space community is still not ready to send humans there. However, a manned mission to Mars is a goal that Dr. Bob Zubrin really believes in.

Dr. Zubrin NASA had plans to send people to Mars by 1981. Those plans were credible. We should have been on Mars a quarter century ago.

Narrator Bob Zubrin is president of the Mars Society, an international organization he helped start in 1998. The Mars Society supports the goal of having humans explore and live on Mars. Its members talk to government agencies and private companies to get money to explore Mars.

Zubrin is also doing research to prepare for a manned mission to Mars. The Mars Society set up living spaces designed for Mars in the deserts of Utah in the western United States, and on Devon Island in northern Canada. These remote areas are similar in some ways to the surface of Mars.

Dr. Zubrin We're trying to find out what field tactics and techniques would be most usefully applied on Mars, what technologies would be most useful to the crew.

Narrator Zubrin has ambitious ideas. He plans to colonize the planet.

Dr. Zubrin We're going to Mars because Mars is the planet that has on it the resources needed to support life and therefore, potentially someday, human civilization.

Narrator For Zubrin, Mars is the new frontier.

Dr. Zubrin Whether or not there has been life on Mars, whether or not there is life on Mars, there will be life on Mars. And it will be us.

Narrator Zubrin isn't the only one with plans for the red planet. Dr. Chris McKay has another idea: He wants to create an atmosphere on Mars so humans can live there.

Dr. McKay If we go to Mars and find that there is no life, then I say we might as well move in.

Narrator McKay believes that for humans to eventually live on Mars, they need to start by warming up its atmosphere.

Dr. McKay Well, we know how to warm up planets. We're doing it on Earth.

Narrator The first step to warming up the planet is putting greenhouse gases into the Martian atmosphere.

Dr. McKay The effect of these gases would be to melt the ice, bring back the atmosphere, and restore Mars to the conditions it was billions of years ago.

Narrator But if humans are going to live on Mars, they're going to need oxygen. Chris McKay has an idea about how to create oxygen on Mars, using tiny organisms called cyano bacteria.

Dr. McKay These organisms are known as cyano bacteria. It's a type of algae, a single-cell type of algae, that has a very long history on Earth. These were the organisms that first made the oxygen. These organisms could do the same thing on Mars. Send them to Mars and ask them to change the world.

Narrator Cyano bacteria—the planet changers! Scientists continue to study Mars, so that one day humans will travel to the red planet. And perhaps someday in the future, humans will live there.

UNIT 7 The Lost World

Edström We've started our two-day journey through the jungle toward the world's largest cave.

We are here to photograph this cave in 360-degree images. You know, we have to descend into vast, empty darkness. I have a cold sensation along my spine feeling like how, how on earth are we going to be able to capture this place?

Just to create one single 360-degree location, we have to take around 400 images. So we're gonna take thousands to be able to cover the whole place.

We're walking through a big, dark cave. We can see nothing but our headlights. And then we see daylight that's actually inside the cave.

It's an absolutely amazing atmosphere. And it's hard to take in. It's breathtaking. And absolutely huge.

They named the first doline, "Watch Out for Dinosaurs." And that's really the feeling you get when you walk inside that place because you emerge from the darkness of the previous passage into this green landscape inside the cave, and you really feel like there could be dinosaurs or some prehistoric creatures living there.

What I want to convey is the feeling of being there, about walking through this pristine, beautiful place, this cave in Vietnam. And making people realize that places like this are part of our heritage that need to be preserved.

UNIT 8 World Music

Narrator Hundreds of people from around the world are arriving in the English countryside. They are coming for a music festival called WOMAD. WOMAD means "world of music, arts, and dance." The artists come to WOMAD to perform traditional music and dance from their cultures in a celebration of world music. One fan of world music is singer and songwriter Peter Gabriel. He co-founded WOMAD in 1980.

Gabriel I had a very personal, practical attraction to what is now "world music." And I would hear all these fantastic things from all over the world, and there were these really stunning voices doing much better than I ever could. So that was really inspiring for me. What I love to see when I go to WOMAD now is so many people being open-minded and listening to music from all over the world.

Narrator Spaccanapoli, an eight-piece band, is coming from Naples, Italy, to perform at WOMAD. The head of the group, Marcello Colasurdo, sings and plays the tambourine.

Colasurdo Spaccanapoli! Ciao!

Narrator He is getting the group ready for its first performance at WOMAD.

Colasurdo My name is Marcello Colasurdo, and I am from Naples. My father taught me to love the tambourine when I was just a young boy.

Narrator The band's music is a combination of folk rock and the music from two traditional Italian dances, the tarantella and tamurriata.

Colasurdo Tamurriata music is like rap. It's a mountain rap, a country rap—it's part of our culture.

Narrator Marcello gets the inspiration for his music from the streets of Naples, where he lives. People here often sing in the street. It can happen at any time and in any place.

Cartman My dear horse, if you climb this mountain, … I'll buy you a new harness with bells.

Narrator For Marcello, everyone on the street is a neighbor, and every street is a stage in his neighborhood in Naples.

Man I passed my note under the door. Get up, beautiful eyes, and take it! And I place it under your door, and I placed it under your door. And I am pacing back and forth… and I am pacing back and forth… Come take it!

Colasurdo OK, grazie.

UNIT 9 Gorilla Toolmakers

Narrator In some ways, gorillas look and act a lot like us. Now there is new evidence that gorillas may also think like us. These incredible photographs show something that some researchers thought was impossible: proof that wild gorillas can think through problems. And like humans, they can make and use tools to solve those problems.

Wildlife Conservation Society scientists Emma Stokes and Thomas Breuer believe this discovery teaches us a lot about the mind of the great ape. Thomas Breuer first observed gorillas using tools. It was a fantastic discovery. The discovery happened here, in Mbeli Bai, in northern Congo. One morning Breuer saw something amazing, and he took a picture of it. A female gorilla named Leah took a stick and used it as a tool. She used the stick to measure the depth of the water before she walked over it. This was an amazing and scientifically important moment.

Breuer When I cross the swamp, I always use a kind of stick to test the water deepness. And what's fascinating is that these gorillas found exactly the same solution to this problem.

Narrator These are the first photographs that show wild gorillas using tools—something no one has ever seen before.

Breuer We know that in the past, we claim that tool use is a unique feature of our own species. But we know that it's not the case any longer. Animals are able to plan. They think and they find a solution to a problem.

Narrator For years now, we've known that some animals use tools. They often use tools to get food. These chimpanzees use clubs to crack open nuts. Then they teach their skills to the next generation. They use sticks to get insects… and they use leaves like cups to scoop up water. But, until now, scientists did not know that wild gorillas also used tools. Some gorillas in zoos use sticks to find bugs. But scientists never saw them do this in the wild.

And there was more. One month later, Breuer was lucky again. He saw a second gorilla inventing a tool. A female named Efi put a branch into the ground. She held onto it as she reached into the water. Apes at Mbeli Bai often hang onto trees in order to pull themselves up from the water. But this gorilla created a tool to stay out of the water. This incredible new evidence shows that gorillas can create and use tools to solve problems, like humans do. Discoveries like this may help us understand our own evolution, how our earliest ancestors learned to solve more difficult problems.

Stokes It just goes to show the kinds of benefits you can see from a long-term research presence in somewhere like Mbeli Bai. We could be here for hundreds of years and still not truly uncover all of the secrets the forests have to offer.

UNIT 10 Photo Camp

Rainier Get down low on the ground and photograph. Get up high, like up here, and shoot down.

Narrator These are some of the best photographers in the world.

Deghati Don't move, don't move.

Narrator They are working with young people who haven't used cameras before.

Deghati She's so happy to see how it's working.

Student Yeah! So happy.

Woman Take one of Justin.

Narrator These young people are refugees. They live in Uganda. They are from many parts of Africa, but right now, this camp is their only home. They don't know what will happen to them in the future. They speak many different languages. But award-winning National Geographic photographer Reza Deghati believes they can all understand the meaning of powerful images.

Deghati Now, I don't speak your language, but I use photography like language, and this is the pictures I take.

Narrator Reza and National Geographic photographers Ed Kashi and Chris Rainier…

Rainier That's a very good shot.

Narrator … have joined South African photographer Neo Ntsoma. They are teaching 60 young refugees how to tell the stories of their lives in photographs.

Deghati This is the way that we say, "telling the stories by picture." What is important for me? What is the good, what is the bad around me? That's how I use the photography.

Narrator The photographers call this Photo Camp.

Deghati Photography is more than just having pictures of your friends standing together.

Narrator In small groups, the young people learn to use cameras and to compose pictures.

Deghati This is more reflections of the trees in this… what you can get.

Narrator Photo Camp is an inspiration for many of the camp residents. Aganze Grace, for example, wants to become a professional photographer. He hopes to take portraits and passport pictures to help support his family.

Deghati You are great! You can be a good photographer.

Narrator Life is difficult in the refugee camp. But Reza and the other photographers are showing these young adults how to see their temporary home in a new way, and perhaps to create something meaningful while they are here. Near the end of the program, the students have an exhibition. They are excited to show their work. As Reza explained to them at the beginning, their pictures tell stories that everyone can understand, no matter where they are from or what language they speak. These students received more than just a certificate and a new skill at Photo Camp.

Ntsoma Wave your certificates!

Narrator They also learned how to document their world and to see themselves and their lives in new ways.

GRAPHIC ORGANIZERS

Unit 1   Life in a Day

Complete the outline as you read *A Day on Planet Earth*.

Who did what? → Film director _____ and his _____ produced a _____ movie called *Life in a Day*.

When? → On a single day: _____

How many? → People in _____ countries uploaded _____ videos to YouTube—more than _____ hours.

Questions the Team Asked   **Some Answers They Received**

What do you _____ most? →
- _____ and _____
- _____ and _____ cars
- a pet _____ and a _____

What do you _____? →
- imaginary _____ and real-life _____
- _____ are going to eat their _____
- guns, _____, the loss of _____

Why was the film possible? → Because of the way people are all _____ in the age of the Internet

Unit 2 Don't Give Up!

Complete the diagram as you read *The World's Oldest First Grader*.

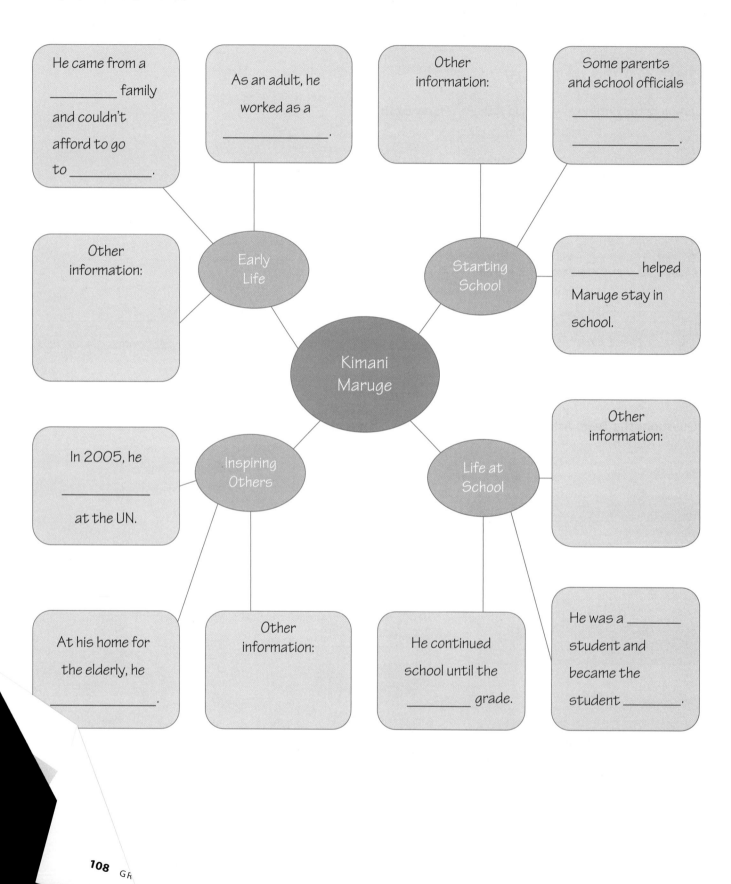

He came from a _____ family and couldn't afford to go to _____.

As an adult, he worked as a _____.

Other information:

Some parents and school officials _____ _____.

Other information:

Early Life

Starting School

_____ helped Maruge stay in school.

Kimani Maruge

In 2005, he _____ at the UN.

Inspiring Others

Life at School

Other information:

At his home for the elderly, he _____.

Other information:

He continued school until the _____ grade.

He was a _____ student and became the student _____.

Unit 3 Why We Buy

Complete the diagram as you read *The Psychology of Supermarkets*.

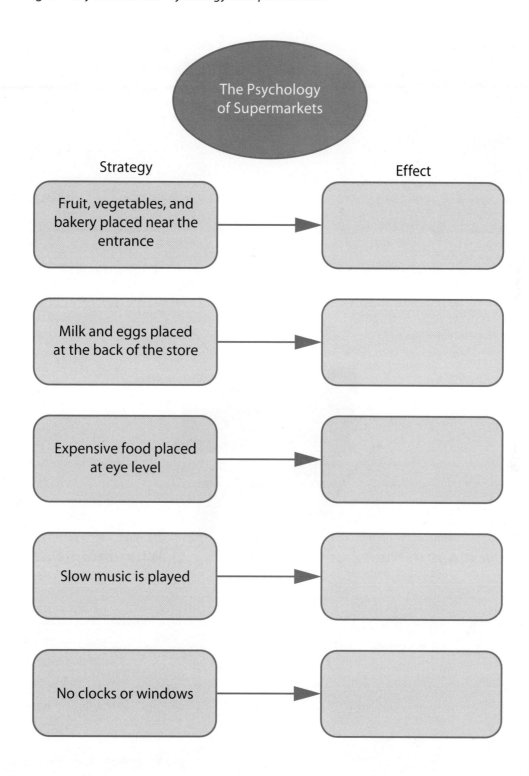

The Psychology of Supermarkets

Strategy

Effect

Fruit, vegetables, and bakery placed near the entrance

Milk and eggs placed at the back of the store

Expensive food placed at eye level

Slow music is played

No clocks or windows

Unit 4 Green Living

Complete the diagram as you read *Garbage Island*.

❶ What it is

- The garbage island is a collection of _____ of pieces of _____ and other everyday objects that people _____.

- Examples of these everyday objects include _____ bags and _____ bottles.

❸ Why it's a problem

- Sea _____ may eat plastic _____ and die.

- Tiny _____ near the ocean surface _____ sunlight from reaching deeper water; lack of _____ kills _____, leaving less food for_____.

❷ How it got there

- Pacific Ocean _____ bring objects together and cause them to _____ around in a giant _____.

- The _____ movement stops the _____ from _____.

- New objects _____ the spinning _____, and the island _____ bigger.

❹ What people are doing

- Environmental engineer _____ is building a _____ that _____ garbage from the ocean.

- Singer Pharrell Williams works with a company that _____ plastic garbage from the ocean into _____ for blue jeans.

Unit 5 Food Journeys

Complete the chart as you read *Cooking the World*. If you can't find the information in the passage, write "not given."

GLOBAL TABLE ADVENTURE	CHOWHOUND	THE AMATEUR GOURMET	SOMEONE ATE THIS	KITCHEN HISTORIC
Who started it?	Who started it?	Who started it?	Who started it?	Who started it?
Why did they start it?	Why did they start it?	Why did they start it?	Why did they start it?	Why did they start it?
What is it about?	What is it about?	What is it about?	What is it about?	What is it about?
Other information:	Other information:	Other information:	Other information:	Other information:

Unit 6 Future Living

Complete the diagram as you read *How Will We Live?*

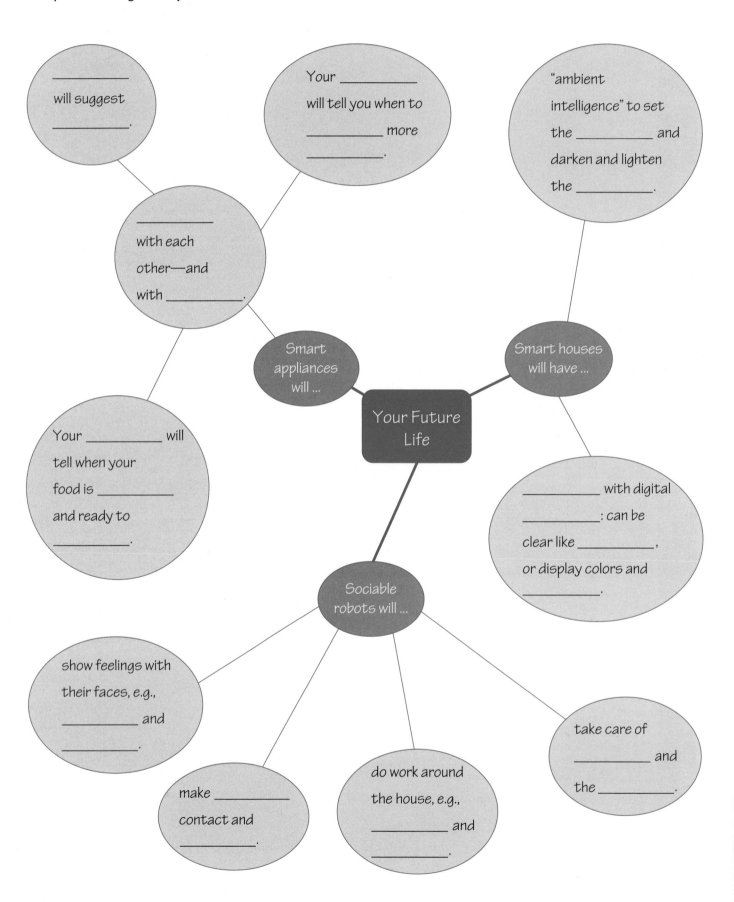

_____ will suggest _____.

Your _____ will tell you when to _____ more _____.

"ambient intelligence" to set the _____ and darken and lighten the _____.

_____ with each other—and with _____.

Your _____ will tell when your food is _____ and ready to _____.

Smart appliances will …

Smart houses will have …

Your Future Life

_____ with digital _____: can be clear like _____, or display colors and _____.

Sociable robots will …

show feelings with their faces, e.g., _____ and _____.

make _____ contact and _____.

do work around the house, e.g., _____ and _____.

take care of _____ and the _____.

Unit 7 Exploration

Complete the diagram as you read *Into the Unknown*.

WHAT IS A BLUE HOLE?

WHERE ARE SOME EXAMPLES?

HOW DEEP CAN THEY GET?

WHAT ARE THE DANGERS OF EXPLORING BLUE HOLES?

WHY DO PEOPLE EXPLORE BLUE HOLES?

Unit 8 Music with a Message

Create a timeline similar to the one below to take notes as you read *Music for Change*. Take notes on either Arn Chorn-Pond or Zinhle Thabethe.

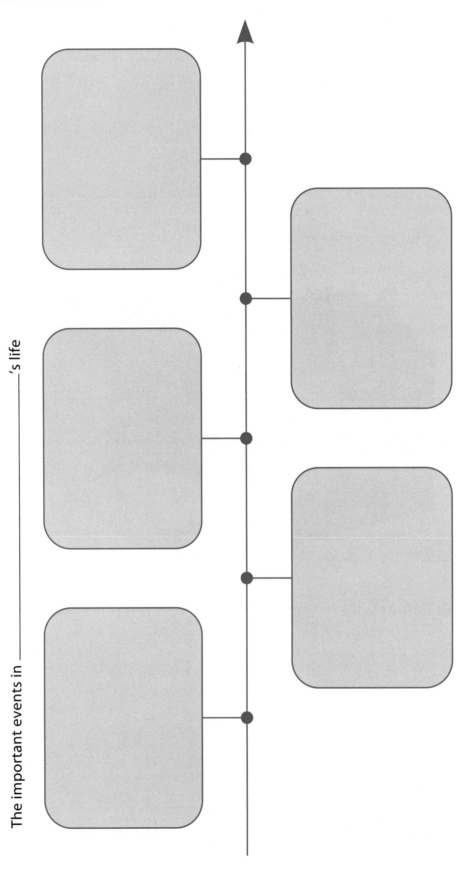

The important events in _____'s life

Unit 9 Animal Behavior

Complete the notes as you read *The Animal Trainer*.

Cesar Millan: an animal _____—helps _____ and dog _____ deal with their _____.

The biggest mistake people make with dogs: We _____ dogs.

Why people like certain kinds of dogs:

It's what people want from _____, but _____. e.g., a pit bull represents _____, _____, and _____.

Millan's approach to helping dog owners:

- If you don't tell a _____ what to _____, it will _____ you what to _____.

- You don't _____ a dog if it would like to go for _____—you put on the _____ and _____.

What his parents think about his work:

- They wanted him to become a _____, like a _____ or _____.

- His father still doesn't understand why people pay him for _____.

What he thinks dogs teach us:

- to _____ in the _____

- _____ (dogs will never _____ to you) and loyalty

Millan believes _____ behave better than _____.

Unit 10 The Power of Images

Complete the information about the photographs as you read *How Photography Connects Us.*

Photographer	What the photo shows	What is special about the image
Brent Stirton	Villagers carrying a silverback _____ named _____ Senkwekwe, who was illegally _____ in the _____ Democratic Republic of Congo in _____ .	The photo had a _____ around the world and made people more aware of the _____ facing wild gorillas.
Randy Olson	A young _____ Mbuti boy getting ready for a _____ , and a young Mbuti _____ behind him.	The photo reminds David Griffin of Degas's bronze _____ of a ballet _____ .
Son Truong	A woman _____ in the Vietnamese countryside while her _____ played on a swing.	The image was taken by an _____ photographer. It shows that _____ has at least one or two great photos in them.